The Marriage of
Sense and Thought

Renewal in Science

The Renewal in Science series offers books that seek to enliven and deepen our understanding of nature and science.

Genetics and the Manipulation of Life: The Forgotten Factor of Context
by Craig Holdrege

The Wholeness of Nature: Goethe's Way toward a Science of Conscious Participation in Nature
by Henri Bortoft

The Marriage of Sense and Thought

Imaginative Participation in Science

Stephen Edelglass

Georg Maier

Hans Gebert

John Davy

 Lindisfarne Books

The Marriage of Sense and Thought is a revised edition (with additions) of *Matter and Mind* (1992).

Copyright © 1997 Lindisfarne Books

This edition published by Lindisfarne Books
3390 Route 9, Hudson, NY 12534

Library of Congress Cataloging-in-Publication Data
The marriage of sense and thought : imaginative participation
in science / Stephen Edelglass ... [et al.]
    p. cm. — (Renewal in science)
Rev. ed. of: Matter and mind. c1992.
Includes bibliographical references and index.
ISBN 0-940262-82-7 (paper)
1. Science—Philosophy. 2. Science—Methodology.
3. Knowledge, Theory of. I. Edelglass, Stephen. II. Matter
and mind. III. Series.
Q175.M373 1997
501—dc21   96-29674
                                                CIP

Cover illustration: Henri Matisse, *Goldfish*, 1912.
Pushkin Musuem of Fine Arts, Moscow, Russia. © 1997 Succession H. Matisse,
Paris/Artists Rights Society (ARS), N.Y.

Cover design: Barbara Richey

Text drawings from Stephen Edelglass, except pp. 126–127, which are
from *In Partnership with Nature* by Jochen Bockemühl, published by
Bio-Dynamic Literature, Wyoming, Rhode Island, 1981.

10 9 8 7 6 5 4 3 2 1

Printed in the United States of America

Contents

Preface to the Second Edition

THIS BOOK WAS FIRST PUBLISHED four years ago with the title *Matter and Mind*. Its present title, *The Marriage of Sense and Thought*, points to the reason for bringing out a new edition. Both titles allude to the cleavage between the inner experience of human consciousness and the outer world of sense. This opposition has been a defining feature of Western experience since the time of Descartes. The new title, however, also suggests that the separation between inner and outer can be transcended. That this gap can be overcome through human participation in the world of phenomena is a main theme of this book.

While the first edition was well received, readers did not always notice that a truly phenomena-based science has radical implications for understanding sense experience and the world of phenomena. The present revised edition is an attempt to remedy that situation. We clarified and amplified those sections on the philosophical supposi- tions underlying imaginative participation in phenomena. *The Marriage of Sense and Thought* remains, however, a book about practice—the practice of gaining knowledge-rich, meaningful experience of the natural world.

STEPHEN EDELGLASS
Chestnut Ridge, New York
GEORG MAIER
Dornach, Switzerland
September 1996

Acknowledgments

We wish to thank Owen Barfield, James Hindes, Robert McDermott, and Brian Stockwell for the thoroughness with which they commented on the first draft of this book. Their valuable insights, generously given, significantly contributed to the final result. We especially wish to thank James Hindes for editing the first edition of this book. His long-standing interest in science and grasp of our intentions enabled him to focus our prose, thereby making the content more accessible to the reader. The second edition has benefited greatly from John Barnes' careful reading. His questions and editorial comments make this new edition clearer and more precise in countless ways. Hanna Edelglass followed the book through all its drafts, reading, listening, and suggesting. That the book is understandable to the general reader is in no small measure due to her. Finally, we wish to thank the Fund for Phenomenological Science for its financial support.

STEPHEN EDELGLASS

Preface

THIS BOOK WAS TRULY COAUTHORED. It is the result of a culture of work that values conversation as a means of making scientific progress. Its conception as a whole and in its individual chapters was a joint effort that evolved over many years. The content of each chapter was planned by the group of authors, written by one of the group, and then rewritten by another after further discussion. And, often, it was rewritten again. Consequently, this book does not consist of separately contributed chapters. To the extent that we have been successful, it is a coherent whole. It was a wonderful experience for me to work in a community where individual gifts contribute toward a totality.

The beginnings of this book go back to the time when, as a young man, I joined the faculty of the Cooper Union for the Advancement of Science and Art in New York City. Increasingly during those early years, I was disturbed by the chasm between the world of professional life and that of inner experience and personal ideals. If science was the method and measure of objective truth, then it seemed as if my personal conduct and humanity were meaningless—in the sense that they were irrelevant not only to a world reality presumed by science as presently practiced but also because personal striving was unrecognized in the results of that same science. I was haunted in this regard by Bertrand Russell's remark: "Morals are like oysters. Some people like them, some people don't." I wanted to discover firmer ground than arbitrary choice for inner struggling. But this, I felt, was precluded by the results and the materialistic worldview of science.

A few years later, while teaching a graduate course in quantum mechanics, I finally saw the fallacy in thinking that science had the last word concerning the nature of reality—that somehow philosophical questions came in the form of trying to understand the results of science, after the fact so to speak, while the presuppositions upon which science was built were left unexamined and taken for granted. Scientific methods and the contemporary scientific paradigm had previously had an aura of logical necessity whose transcendence seemed, until that time, unthinkable. With this realization I felt freed to explore new possibilities.

As I undertook a search to discover if a science that bridged the gulf between inner and outer experience was possible, I was fortunate to meet several scientists who were concerned with similar questions. Hans Gebert, whom I met in 1973, shared ideas and worked together with me for many years. Until 1985 he was the co-director of the Waldorf Institute of Mercy College in Detroit and before that Director of the Physics Laboratory at the Birmingham (England) Technical College.

Not many years after I met Hans, I attended a series of lectures on human physiology given by John Davy. It was a thrill to see questions examined freshly—not out of assumptions, but out of examined experience. Hans and I invited John to join our work. At that time John Davy was vice principal of Emerson College in Forest Row, England. Before that he had been the science editor of the English national newspaper *The Observer.*

And, finally, ten years ago John introduced me, much to my good fortune and gratitude, to Georg Maier. Georg gave up neutron diffraction research in Aachen, Germany, in order to pursue research into modes of observation and conceptualization of nature at the *Forschungslaboratorium am Goetheanum* in Dornach, Switzerland.

On October 28, 1984, well before the completion of this work, John Davy died as the consequence of a malignant brain tumor. Before he knew he was ill he had concerned himself with Elisabeth Kübler-Ross's ideas concerning the stages of death and dying, relating them to other life experiences. It was at this time that John wrote *Discovering Hope*. His death was an inspiration to many, as was the way he lived his life. It is to him that this book is dedicated.

STEPHEN EDELGLASS

Threefold Educational Foundation
Spring Valley, New York
March 1991

1. Two Smiles

When friends meet, they smile. They greet one another warmly and are glad to have met again. These sentences describe a common event in a simple and comprehensible way. But they are not "scientific." The warmth of a greeting cannot be measured by a thermometer, nor is the accompanying "gladness" observable. How then could friendship be described scientifically?

Such a description might begin with the observation that a smile is a widening of the oral aperture, caused by contractions of the cheek musculature. A "scientific" investigation of such a meeting between friends might further consider the physiological changes within the body, especially the effect on the brain, although an investigation of that sort would probably be too complex to expect any useful results. At best, studies might be centered on the ethological functions of smiles, their possible relationship to placatory action patterns found in situations of potentially aggressive behavior in other higher vertebrates. We could also undertake to analyze how various reinforcement schedules may affect the frequency and intensity of oral aperture widening in different human subjects.

The fact that we can describe a smile as a smile or as the widening of an oral aperture points both to the reason for this book and to two serious and related questions that we propose to explore. The first question is, What does it mean that our scientific culture, which is so extraordinary and powerful, can talk about human beings only in a dehumanizing way? Most of our ordinary ways of talking about human life are more or less comprehensible, but entirely unscientific. The attempt to make them scientific produces results, as in the preceding paragraph, that most sensible people would recognize as bizarre, if not absurd. Apparently, in order to speak "scientifically" we must either stop talking about human life or make it virtually unrecognizable.

The second question derives from the first: Can we do anything about this situation? Is the conclusion to be drawn from our dichotomous culture that we should discipline our minds and language so that we not only describe a smile as the widening of an oral aperture but also *see* it as such? Must we accept this split culture, in which each half speaks nonsense to the other? In this book we propose to examine science itself and, by tracing the origins of this strange dichotomy, to show a way in which the split can be overcome.

We are not the first to ask these questions, of course, or to attempt to form some answers. But we have rarely found them discussed in the context of "human faculties." This is our starting point, because science arises through the use of certain human faculties that have been schooled in the practice of science. Since science as we know it is only a few hundred years old, people in prescientific times must have either used different faculties or used the same faculties differently. We shall therefore look at the emergence of what is known as "modern science," its passage through several revolutions, and its present condition and possible future. We shall do this while constantly bearing in mind that we are talking about expressions of human faculties—notably thinking and imagination—which are complex and mysterious. We shall try to remain aware that any description of science, whether of its history or its present character, is based upon an implicit assumption concerning the nature of knowing. Such assumptions, although they may be founded on concepts that are in themselves clear, are seldom explicitly described. Nevertheless, we cannot know what is known if we ignore the knower.

In chapter two we shall examine the basis of the "materialism" that dominates both modern scientific thinking as it is usually practiced and, perhaps more importantly, most of our ordinary ways of imagining the world. Then, in chapter three, we shall examine how the ideas of physical science evolved and attempt to discern the changing attitudes that developed toward them. In the final chapters we shall sketch a possible way that science can develop in which both the nature of knowing and the use of human faculties are not forgotten, but actually included.

The Scientific View

Developing further our two opening questions, let us consider some of the curious features of scientific language. Why does it seem unscientific to speak of a "warm smile"? A simple assertion that this kind of warmth cannot be measured, that the word is being employed as a metaphor for an emotional state, is not enough. The claim that science deals in facts, not metaphors, is insufficient; many words in our language, including those whose primary use is scientific, have metaphorical as well as literal meanings. Besides, emotional states are facts just as much as the smiles that express them. The question really hinges on what is meant by "an emotional state." Do we mean an "inner" experience, as we know it within ourselves and infer it in others? Or do we mean a variety of physiological events that might be registered by instruments—changes in pulse rate, blood flow, electrical resistance of the skin, brain waves, and so on? A strictly behavioristic program would allow only the latter and urge that all words referring to "inner" experiences be eliminated from scientific language. Thus, we would have to give up saying "he is hungry" and remark instead that "he is exhibiting rapid eating behavior" or "my endoscope shows that his stomach is empty."

The results of rigidly adhering to such a discipline would be strained and ludicrous as far as ordinary life is concerned. Nevertheless, the behavioristic approach draws our attention to a feature of the scientific attitude generally regarded as essential: total objectification. This stance is purportedly achieved by setting aside all personal experiences, all feelings, desires, prejudices—in short, all personal involvement—in order to achieve a completely objective and impersonal relationship to the world. Since they cannot be observed in others, inner experiences must be banned. Even though we can observe our own inner experiences, such introspection produces nothing but private knowledge about private events. Science, however, is concerned with public knowledge of public realities. From here it is only a step to the wholesale dismissal of all inner experiences as illusory or nonexistent. Actually, for large parts of the natural world our culture has already effected this. We do not think of a mineral or plant as having an inner life; even animals are treated as though they had no feeling. Indeed, we are on the way to treating human beings in some circumstances as though they did not have real inner lives either.

There are, of course, a great many knotty problems buried in this rather simple account of science. In the course of this work we hope to unravel a few of them. At this stage we simply wish to characterize in a nontechnical way the background picture that permeates the very way we think about science and the scientific attitude. In this picture we see that a decision has already been made concerning which kinds of experience we will attend to; for example, we have regard for "objective" phenomena, but not for "subjective" feelings. We are prepared to exercise the use of certain faculties, such as detachment, but not others, such as empathy.

It is generally accepted that science entails an effort to be "objective." But it is not generally realized that such science is based upon assumed notions concerning the nature of the universe, notions settled upon before any description or discussion even begins. The most primary and obvious of such notions is that the universe consists essentially of "objects." Hence, science's pursuit of truth required the "objectification" of that which it would study. Already the plant and mineral worlds have been largely reduced to "objects" for such study. Attitudes toward the animal and human worlds are not yet consistent in this regard. Nevertheless, science's search for ultimate realities assumes that in the end they will turn out to consist of impersonal events, not personal feelings, and of objects, rather than beings. In ordinary conversation we may persist in speaking of our inner experiences as though they were realities. But we do not expect such experiences to be revealed as ultimate constituent parts of the universe. This expectation is, of course, totally opposite to that of earlier, prescientific approaches to knowledge, in which the ultimate realities of the universe were sought not in impersonal objects but in personal beings. It is widely considered a major triumph of science to have transcended these superstitions by recognizing them for what they are: projections of our inner life out into the "real" universe. Hence, for real knowledge to be attainable, the "outer world" had to be purged of this inner life.

Yet we seldom seem to notice the irony of the situation we have thereby created. Having eliminated beings from the universe, we have eliminated ourselves as well. We achieve this end by exercising detached observation, but we forget to ask who or where this detached observer is. We seem to hang around in some kind of ghostly realm looking at a universe in which we ourselves cannot exist. This model of knowing goes back to Descartes, who formulated in crystal clear concepts a development that began with the Greek philosophers and led to a division of the universe into *res extensa* and *res cogitans*—which we rather loosely call "matter" and "mind." The Cartesian universe is partitioned into the objects of sense experience and the world of thought.

The notion of the detached observer thus emerges from a slightly spooky way of imagining the universe: Scientists see the world as a machine, which they haunt like ghosts. Since the idea of a detached observer seems to call for attentiveness, but otherwise for no mental work, the scientist is actually a rather passive ghost. Yet one of the experiences common to all scientists is that of intense mental work—indeed, work that takes place within the mind, the very realm with no existence in the objective universe.

Descartes himself had a powerful awareness of this activity. His own mental effort provided him with an experience of self so immediate and independent of the world outside himself that he felt he could base the certainty of his own existence upon it: *Cogito, ergo sum*, "I think, therefore I am." Western philosophy has tended to accept the Cartesian dichotomy of mind and matter while forgetting the active ego who discovers it. This dichotomy is widely and rightly recognized as a pivotal notion in the development of modern science. But we should remember its genesis: a thinking subject discovered it in a strenuous and highly individualized effort. We must not forget that the work of generating impersonal knowledge about the universe of objects, not beings, is accomplished by beings, not objects. Granted that the nature of scientific inquiry is to achieve an impersonal understanding of the world, still, important questions remain. What is the nature of the highly personal work of the scientist in achieving knowledge? What does the effort itself signify? Where and how does the scientist do it? These are questions we will be examining in later chapters.

Another inviolate assumption of science is this: In principle it is possible for any individual to make discoveries about the universe. This assumption is so much taken for granted that we often forget how revolutionary, not to say heretical, it was when first posited. It is customary to present high-school science students with stories of the early martyrs of the scientific age. These martyrdoms are usually described in terms of a clash between two views of the world. But one of the main aspects of this clash is usually left out. It was not just two views of how the world was made but two views of how knowledge itself is to be obtained. By and large, knowledge in the prescientific age was not seen as an individual's quest for new discoveries, but rather as the receiving of revelation, whether from sages, spiritual leaders, oral traditions, or old books. Occasionally, an individual might personally receive revelations by grace, but the preparation for such grace did not consist of any striving for knowledge. More likely, the grace of knowledge resulted from adequate moral purification. Today we regard the moral life of physicists as a private affair. (Whether we can continue with this assumption will be considered later.) Yet we take it for granted that their professional work will include strenuous intellectual effort, which, though individual and uniquely their own, will lead to impersonal knowledge. By "impersonal" we also mean that their discoveries will be describable in ways that others can grasp and test in a public world of experiment.

We are, of course, talking about the essence of any science that can be described as genuine. Science put forward as dogma, as obscure rigmarole, as formulas to be learned by rote is not real science at all. The experience of scientific insight demands *personal activity*. Although we know this, we continue the ironic demand that science confine itself to producing impersonal descriptions of the universe with no place for the scientists who actually produce them. In this book we hope to bring into focus certain traditional ways of thinking about scientific work and the world scientists "discover." These ways of thinking float as assumptions in the background of much ordinary talk about science, and, because the assumptions are seldom explicit, the ironic situation they create remains unnoticed.

Inner Experience and the Outer Environment

Behind the strange notion of individual scientists achieving knowledge of a universe in which they do not exist lies the experience of the Cartesian dichotomy: consciousness is *always* of something *other* than the one who is conscious. This is what we all experience when we wake up in the morning and emerge from dream consciousness. The original unity of our I-world splits into a dichotomy when we start thinking actively about the world presented to our awakened senses.

It is an immediate fact of experience that the perceived world appears to be "out there," while I myself, with my personal feelings and memories, am "in here." From my private world I look out into what seems to be a public world, existing separately from me. My waking in the morning brings me into separation, into alienation.

This dichotomy prompts many questions, chief among which is, Can I grasp "in here" what is going on "out there"? If I assume that this is possible (which is the *sine qua non* of the scientific endeavor), I am also assuming that the dichotomy in which I find myself can somehow, to some degree, be transcended. Furthermore, such transcendence would mean that the private world of my mind and the public world are not ultimately of two kinds, but share common ground. This question of how the two worlds are related has troubled philosophers for a long time. The standard solution has been to categorize one side of the dichotomy as illusory: my side. Of course, this still leaves me as the ghost haunting the world machine (perhaps even haunting the widening oral apertures). Another, less fashionable solution in Western culture is for me to eliminate the world "out there," concluding that it is all my dream. Setting aside these radical solutions, it is encouraging that we are not, in fact, afflicted by philosophical doubts when we awake in the morning. We see people who appear to be like ourselves strenuously trying to understand the world and live in it. This endeavor suggests that a hope and an expectation still live in most of us that the dichotomy is at least partly resolvable.

We leave this as an initial response to the first of our two leading questions: Why does science have to speak about the world in a dehumanizing way? As we have seen, science grows out of a real dichotomy of experience, which is, to begin with, that we ourselves are observers detached from our surroundings. Furthermore, it is important to bear in mind that we ourselves generate this dichotomy. Upon waking we use certain faculties in certain ways.

Thus, we can add a further perspective to the second question. Granted that we cannot completely convince ourselves that the universe which we ourselves have discovered has no place for us, what can we do about it? That something needs to be done about it becomes more obvious every year. If we systematically think of a world in which human beings don't exist, we should not be surprised to find ourselves creating a world in which they can't exist. In the first half of this century it was still common to find idealistic and intelligent people who saw science as the great enlightener. They thought applied science would soon bring solutions to the world's great problems, even though there would always be cranks who were doubtful, who nagged about the environment, armaments, and computers. The ideas of people like E. F. Schumacher about the coming energy crisis, the irrelevance of our technology to the Third World, and the need for conservation, for appropriate scale, for human technology, and so on seemed eccentric and irrelevant to the times.

Of course, a great deal of techno-optimism still exists. It continues to inspire much political and economic language which sees growth and technical advance as the essential key to our human future. Yet a profound skepticism has also made its appearance, and it has been growing. We can no longer seriously maintain that advanced Western societies are in good health physically, mentally, or emotionally or that they have a sound and balanced relationship to the earth's natural resources or to other human communities. And within our society, a malaise is apparent, which can best be described as a loss of meaning.

We should not find this situation surprising, for we are trained through education and the habitual thought forms of a scientific culture to practice detachment, objectivity, and the elimination of inwardness when dealing with the public world. As a detached observer one not only becomes detached from the world but also gradually loses touch with oneself and others as personal beings. A good deal of inner desperation ensues. Some recovery of meaning may be possible through weekend encounter groups, personal growth workshops or religious cults and revivals, but those solutions do not help one as a scientist.

Against this background many people, especially the young, turn away from practicing science and even worse, from thinking scientifically. Such rejection is very bad for our civilization for, as we hope to show, our very sense of individual independence and freedom arose through the exercise of such thinking. And now, ironically, we see that this kind of thinking is also responsible for our experience of loss of meaning. Faced with this paradox we ask, Is it really necessary for scientific thinking to be devoid of human spiritual value?

The authors are convinced that true science was and still can be a profound spiritual adventure, which is only in its beginnings. But its real nature has been lost, obscured, even eliminated by a kind of sclerosis. For this illness of science we must find a cure that will begin only when science recognizes that it originates in the use of specific human faculties. We need to look more deeply into the origins and development of these faculties—past, present, and future. We can no longer afford to live with a nonsensical world picture produced by human beings that does not include human beings in their wholeness and richness. We need a science that can embrace the warmth of smiles as well as the muscular contractions that widen oral apertures, that can include the inwardness of all the kingdoms of nature, of human beings, and of the universe as a whole. Our search for such a science will begin with a careful look at the origins of classical science.

2. The Deeper Roots of Materialism

Materialism is not a sharply defined philosophy, but a habit of mind pervading our culture and deeply influencing its science. Stated most simply, materialism is the view that the universe consists ultimately of matter. Examined more closely, however, it soon reveals itself as a collection of loosely associated experiences, assumptions, and beliefs. Materialism is usually closely associated with reductionism; physics is assumed to be more fundamental than chemistry, chemistry more fundamental than biology, and biology more fundamental than psychology. Mind is regarded as an epiphenomenon of matter and the human being as "ultimately" a consequence of very complex "physical" processes and laws. Hence, materialism dismisses as superstition the prescientific conviction that the ultimate realities of the universe are not things, but beings. This dismissal is supported by more than a habit of mind; the beings that apparently peopled the medieval and earlier universes are not to be seen in the world around us. Unobservable today, such beings must have been "imagined" and not "real."

This common and natural modern objection to prescientific cosmologies points to another element in materialism: the assumption that explanatory conceptions of the universe must be based on what we can observe. To most people this means observations by means of physical senses. We say that "seeing is believing." Our doubts concerning the reality of anything are put to rest if it is solid and tangible.

Although they have learned from childhood that seeing and touching are the most important means of testing material reality, scientists in our century have had to become used to the fact that most of the "realities" now being explored, especially in physics and chemistry, cannot be seen or touched by the unaided senses. Specially designed instruments are required. Nevertheless, we still habitually employ words and concepts drawn from sense experience, even when speaking about the invisible and intangible realms now under investigation. In high-energy physics, where the materialistic paradigm is most obviously out of date, this is quite striking. The words we hear, "particles," "particle accelerators," "targets," and so on, seem to imply that the objects described would be both visible and tangible if they were not so small. Yet on reflection, scientists realize there is no meaningful way the realms they are exploring can be described as either visible or tangible. Their discourse includes many words, such as "fields" and "quanta" of energy, that, as images, are far less material. Yet even though the images implied in their materialistic language are partly transcended by the more abstract mathematical expressions of current theory, as a habit of mind science continues to be imbued with qualities and concepts derived from earlier stages of its development. The all-pervading idea of "conservation" is just one example.

It could perhaps be said that twentieth-century science can no longer be described as "materialistic" because it no longer sees the universe as consisting ultimately of material objects, however small. Still, other elements of the materialistic outlook persist: for example, although scientists may no longer expect to find ultimate particles in any material sense, the universe is nevertheless still thought of as impersonal. When high-energy physicists speak of the "flavor" of particles, they are not implying that they can taste them. Nor do they imagine that particles with "flavor" or "charm" are particularly attractive to one another. (Why essentially mathematical properties should be given such whimsical names is an interesting psychological question in itself.) Moreover, the reductionistic assumption that human thoughts and feelings can be reduced to functions of impersonal particles, forces, and laws persists, not only in scientific circles but also in our civilization at large.

We shall examine the situation of twentieth-century science more fully in the next chapter. Our intention at this stage is merely to point out the habitual frame of reference within which science operates and to show how popular science and most science education today are permeated with concepts and language almost a century out of date. The science that began with Galileo, Descartes, and their contemporaries and came to an end with the nineteenth century is the framework for what we shall call classical science. This frame of reference needs to be examined more carefully. A better understanding of science will enable us to tackle the problems of alienation and loss of meaning from a new point of view.

Materialism is more than a habit in our society. Sometimes subtly, other times overtly, it exerts a force much as religious doctrine did in past ages. Many people in Western cultures—particularly educated people—feel nervous and uncomfortable when confessing to any belief in nonmaterial realities, especially so if asked to describe spiritual, religious, or paranormal experiences (for example, an encounter with the soul of a departed relative). They know that if they appear to take such experiences as real—that is, as "objective" realities—they risk being regarded as mentally unbalanced. A kind of private compartment of the mind containing "religious beliefs" is more or less permissible, even respectable. But such beliefs are regarded as private concerns, whereas science is concerned with public and universal realities. Science now functions in society rather as the Church did in the Middle Ages. It is heresy to doubt that science is the guardian of the most essential and well-established truths.

Space, Matter, Time, Force, Energy

We suggested in the first chapter that the most powerful reason for the emergence of the "detached observer" lies in actual experience. We wake in the morning and seem to find two different realities, the private world of our thoughts, feelings, memories, and intentions "in here," which we experience as completely detached from a world of things "out there." In a similar way we would expect to find definite experiences behind the doctrine of materialism. The gap between the experiences and the doctrine is bridged by concepts; some of the most basic of these we will now examine.

The materialistic worldview is constructed from space, matter (primarily solid bodies having mass), time, and force or energy. The materialist is happiest with a world of solid bodies moving in space and time. Bodies moving relative to one another can be observed and described mathematically. Their motion can be followed by a detached observer who merely records events and has no part in the collisions of particles or changes in their speed or direction. In his *Dialogues Concerning Two New Sciences* (1632), Galileo aimed at giving such a picture in the second science he described. We call it a *kinematic picture of the world*, a world purely "out there," with no human beings and no explanations, merely descriptions.

Without realizing it, however, the materialistic scientist does go beyond mere observation, participating unconsciously in the moving solid bodies. Indeed, it is just such personal involvement that allows us to ascribe to concepts such as mass, force, energy, inertia, and so forth, any meaning at all. Although the scientific establishment has been trying from the beginning to strip these concepts of their anthropomorphic origins, such scientific terms do actually originate in human experiences. The concept of force is derived from our experience of exerting forces and having forces exerted upon us. We know what it feels like to make an effort in order to get a cart moving, to lift a weight, to get any body to move or change its motion. The effort we must make is to a large extent determined by some property of the body which seems closely connected to its weight. There is a difference between stopping a relatively light tennis ball and stopping a heavy brickbat thrown at us. Our unconscious, intuitive sense for the meaning of scientific terms that are "objective" and "out there" arose from *within* us. Our personal experiences lead us to identify, unconsciously, with the objects or particles involved in a collision. Without being aware of it, we actually imagine the forces they exert on each other owing to their speed and what we call their mass.

A kinematic picture of the world with certain human aspects thought back into it we call a *dynamic picture of the world.* The primary concepts that make this transformation possible are force and mass. Closely connected with these two is the concept of energy: we get tired when we make an effort, when we apply forces; when we work in the world, we need energy to resist our tiredness.

Wherever possible, scientists try to replace a dynamic picture with a kinematic one. Consider, for example, the concept of energy: the energy of a moving solid body is connected with its mass, velocity, and position. Having found a mathematical way to express this connection, science limits itself to situations in which neither mass nor energy changes. We speak of the laws of conservation of mass and of energy. Having determined mass and energy at one instant, we can follow the subsequent motion of the body using nothing more than the kinematic concepts of position and velocity in space and time; it is no longer necessary to investigate the forces that cause the changes in position and velocity.

In the preceding paragraphs we described how kinematics replaced dynamics using the example of the laws of conservation of mass and energy. Our description is not the usual one. Ordinarily it is said that the conservation laws have been "discovered." But there is another way to look at the origin and development of classical science. We shall make a case for our description in the next chapter. As we shall make clear, instead of discovering laws, scientists often select situations for discussion that can be simplified to such an extent that they are amenable to treatment by relatively simple mathematics. But now we shall show how the materialistic worldview selected a limited set of perceptions for attention and ignored others. It was this narrowing of what was considered significant that led the new way of doing science to its successes.

The Craftsman and the Scholar

The distinction between merely observing the world of matter and identifying with it, between kinematics and dynamics, is crucial for an understanding of the origins of classical science. These two extremes came together when two ways of life, the scholar's and the craftsman's, met. With the close of the Middle Ages, literate craftsmen appeared who were able to publish some of the secrets of their trades and guilds. An example is *On Pyrotechnics*, published in 1540 by the Italian metalworker Vannoccio Biringuccio. This treatise gives a comprehensive account of the smelting of metals, the casting of cannons and cannon balls, and the making of gunpowder. Men who worked with their hands were beginning to make their skills conscious, to reflect on and describe them in general terms. At the same time, scholars were emerging from their cloisters to become involved in the world of material action. Galileo, a scholarly professor of mathematics at the University of Padua, was beginning to show an intense interest in experiment.

The distinction lives on today, not only in the contrast between kinematics and dynamics, but also in the difference between pure and applied science, between theory and experiment. Gifted theoreticians are not necessarily talented experimenters and vice versa. Yet their interdependence is clear and recognized; each embodies a contrasting mode of learning about the universe, contemplative or active, cerebral or manual. The pure scientist can trace his activity through the universities and cloisters back to the intellectual elite of Greek society, the philosophers, and further back to the Mystery temples and schools of the ancient world. This tradition is well recorded, having been from early times articulate and, at least since Greek times, literate.

The ancestry of the applied scientist disappears in the oral traditions and secrecy of the medieval craft guilds, but we catch curious glimpses from earlier times. In the Old Testament we read that when King Solomon wanted to build his temple, he had to enlist the aid of Hiram. Solomon was the priest-king, the lawgiver, and the theoretician of temple building. He received a revelation of the temple plan, complete with exact dimensions, directly from God. But to realize it, he had to call upon people with "cunning" in working metals and wood, namely, Hiram and his master craftsmen. Throughout history the craft tradition, by its nature, has been concerned with manipulating matter. For thousands of years before the dawn of the scientific age, wood, stone, fibers, and metals had given human beings an understanding of the properties of material substances sufficient for the purpose of very refined practical operations.

The conceptual and mathematical skills at the disposal of the Greeks were entirely adequate for them to have anticipated Galileo and Johannes Kepler by two thousand years or more. But they were not interested in practical applications. From the time of Pythagoras until the end of the Middle Ages, scholars and intellectuals were mainly occupied with other questions. Their attention was directed toward spiritual worlds, since the material world was considered not worthy for free men to work in. That is why slaves were necessary to sustain Greek and Roman culture. The central issue for philosophy was how the human soul might find knowledge of, and a relationship with, the spiritual world. Pythagoras sought this through mathematics and music, Plato, through recollecting the archetypal world that the soul knew before birth. The scholars of the Middle Ages devoted themselves to the reconciliation of individual thought with religious revelation and doctrine.

Scientific materialism was born out of the ability to conceptualize those aspects of the world that craftsmen had known empirically for millennia. Working with solid bodies, which occupied space and were sometimes quite heavy, they knew very well that operating with matter required both time and energy. The elements of materialism we characterized earlier with the abstract words *space, matter, time, force,* and *energy* were the concrete content of everyday experience for the craft worker. So when Galileo began to conceptualize some of these "concrete abstractions" by framing them mathematically, he had at hand a variety of craft instruments, some of them of his own design: rulers for measuring space, scales for weighing matter, and clocks for measuring time. The fundamental work of the physical sciences during the fifteenth and sixteenth centuries was to penetrate conceptually and mathematically the phenomena of space, matter, and energy. Galileo's last book, *Dialogues Concerning Two New Sciences* (1638), was a direct result of that work. The first science he discusses is an aspect of what is now called materials science, the behavior of matter under stress as it is deformed until it breaks. Galileo's treatment of the subject was based on his experience among the artisans of Venice. The second science was, as mentioned earlier, kinematics.

Let us now consider our own concrete experience of the basic elements of materialistic reality. Although space, time, matter, energy, and mass may sound very abstract, they are known, even to the most abstracted scholar, simply through living in a physical body. From birth onward, our lives include a continuous education in elementary applied physics. Within a few weeks of birth, babies spend most of their waking hours manipulating physical objects, including their own physical bodies. They acquire first-hand experience of solid objects in three-dimensional space. A wooden block has a greater mass than balls made of wool, and there is a striking difference between them when the laws of momentum are explored. Sitting, standing up, climbing trees, and playing on seesaws all bestow upon the growing child an extensive empirical knowledge of the laws of leverage and basic mechanics; these are mastered in practice long before we can understand them conceptually. (Jean Piaget, the Swiss psychologist, is particularly known for his pioneering study on the emergence of fundamental concepts in children.)

The Relation of Materialism to Sense Experience

The experience just described is possible only because we have certain senses that make us aware of conditions in our own body. Two such senses are touch and balance. Definite nerves in the skin mediate the sense of touch, while three semicircular canals at right angles to one another in the ear constitute the organs for our sense of

vestibular system.

proprioception

balance. A third widely recognized sense is often called the kinesthetic sense. It allows us to be aware of the positions and motions of parts of our own bodies. We know, for example, how our fingers move even with our hands "hidden" behind our backs. This sense is mediated by organs located in the tendons that link muscles to the skeleton. We would like to describe a fourth sense, the existence of which was pointed out by Rudolf Steiner. Again, it is easiest to recognize in a small child who reacts strongly to hunger, thirst, and other conditions of the body. This is the sense that enables us to be aware of our bodily well-being, or lack of same, in a general way. We shall call it the "somatic" sense.

In spite of the fact that the sense of touch merely tells us that pressure is being exerted on the skin, it can also tell us something about our surroundings. The educator A. C. Harwood described how his daughter, when shown a pocket watch she was not allowed to touch, said, "I want to see it; I want to see it," and tried to reach for it with her hands. When it was pointed out to her that she could already see it, she said, "But I want to see it with my hands." That is, she wanted to "be in touch" with the watch, by feeling its surface and by viewing it from different perspectives according to her own intent. In other words, she wanted to be involved with the watch, to be*hold* it, rather than to merely look at it.

In contrast to touch, it may at first seem that the other three senses—namely, balance, the kinesthetic sense, and the somatic sense—apply only to the body. By describing these senses in more detail, we shall show, however, that the ideas of space, matter, time, force, and energy are closely connected with and are ultimately derived from our experience of all four "body senses."

The Sense of Touch

Let us now examine more closely the experience of touch. The nerves enabling us to sense the things we touch are located mainly in the skin, with the greatest concentrations in sensitive areas such as fingertips and lips. To begin with, touch informs me that I have a skin, a surface that defines me as a physical body; I get to know myself as a topological entity. At this point there is no awareness that I have volume or mass or that there is a three-dimensional space existing beyond my own surface.

It is very important to realize that the sense of touch functions only when something else is also touching the toucher. Something must impinge upon my skin, even if it is only another part of my own body, as when I touch two fingertips together. Awareness of my own surface is kindled when it meets another surface. I become aware of both as surfaces because they come into contact but do not interpenetrate. Together they *define separateness.* Hence, the sense of touch gives an experience that, when conceptualized, tells us about the phenomenon of separateness in the world. Touch speaks to me immediately and directly of a reality "out there," distinct from "my" reality. The sensation of touch engenders the awareness of a realm of otherness and hence of my own separateness. I become aware of myself as a separate entity by touching surfaces that are not "me."

We can learn something from a comparison of the sense of touch with the sense of warmth and cold, which also uses organs located in the skin. There is a famous experiment often cited to show the superiority of thermometers to our sense of temperature. The left hand is placed in a bowl of hot water, the right hand in a bowl of cold water. After a few minutes both hands are placed in a bowl of lukewarm water. At first the tepid water feels cold to the left hand and warm to the right hand. Soon, however, both hands report the same tepid temperature. This experiment shows that the sense of warmth is dependent upon our own relationship to the environment. There is a constant exchange of warmth between the body and its surroundings that makes scientific detachment difficult, if not impossible.

We would like to mention in passing that the usual conclusions drawn from this demonstration are quite superficial. The same experiment repeated with thermometers does not show how hopelessly subjective human hands are compared with scientific instruments. In the last stage, when the thermometers are placed into the lukewarm water, they behave in a fashion very similar to human hands: something different happens to each. In one a column of mercury shrinks; in the other it lengthens. The opposite movements end only when the thermometers, like human hands, have adjusted and both register the same temperature. The only advantage of the thermometer is its scale, which makes it possible to link the positions of a mercury column to numbers.

The results of these "thought experiments" are difficult to express with precision because our language is involved with the perceptions of all our senses. The effort to describe one sense that has been artificially isolated would, for precision, call for the invention of an artificial language. Nevertheless, we hope the point of our exercise is clear: the materialistic outlook includes qualities directly related to touch but not, at least not directly, to warmth. The fact that the feeling of warmth is always based on a dynamic relationship in which we gain or lose heat makes it problematic for the materialistic outlook of the detached observer. Since touching immediately establishes separateness, it does not present such a dilemma. In touching, I constantly reestablish my own detachment. In feeling temperature, I experience an aspect of my physical being that is related to a world in which I am an active participant, not just an onlooker.

The Somatic Sense

Next we consider the sense that brings awareness of the general physiological state of the organism: the "somatic sense." When healthy, we have a dim feeling of well-being that extends throughout our body but is mainly centered in the trunk. We feel the air filling a space in our chest as we inhale, and we feel this space contracting as we exhale. If we eat too much, we feel the fullness of a volume in our abdomen. When not well, we may even feel the position of organs that hurt. Our body image includes not only a surface but also a volume, contained by the skin, occupying its own portion of space. All the sensations of my body contents, when taken together, provide me with an intuition or a direct apprehension of what is meant by the words *volume, bulk,* or *extension.* We are able to understand this fundamental property of solid bodies moving in space only because we ourselves live in a body with extension.

The somatic sense also provides a feeling of mass or weight. We are not usually aware of the mass or weight of our own bodies. Only when ill or when recovering from a recent illness or when tired, do we experience our limbs as "heavy." Yet when we move or lift external bodies, it is the somatic sense that tells us what the effort is costing. If I put a shoulder to a car to get it moving, my effort, experienced by the somatic sense, is commensurate with the mass of the car. When I am hit and thereby stop a moving ball, the pain is a measure of the mass and speed of the external body.

The somatic sense and the sense of touch provide us with the two intuitive experiences necessary to conceptualize one of the essential ingredients of the materialistic outlook: the notion of a material body (whether a planet, a billiard ball, or a speck of dust). Such material bodies are defined by a surface and have mass in some measure. The materialistic outlook sees the universe as made up of such entities. Yet the origin of this world picture is not to be found in observation of the surrounding world, the world "out there," as is commonly assumed, but rather in our experience of our own world, "in here." We know mass and volume through participation in the processes inside our bodies and by our interaction with other bodies. We know the boundaries of our own bodies and of bodies outside us through the sense of touch.

In experiments to test possible reactions of being in space, astronauts were deprived of various sense perceptions, including the somatic sense and the sense of touch. Such sensory deprivation experiences often led to bizarre and alarming disorders of the body image. Some subjects felt their limbs floating away from their bodies or one leg reaching across the room to terminate in a giant foot. Experiments of this type point out how important our senses are for sustaining our normal relationship to the material world, notably to our own bodies.

The Kinesthetic Sense

The kinesthetic sense gives me a direct apprehension of the movements I can make by virtue of having musculature and a skeleton. Through this sense I become aware of my body, not just as a volume with mass enclosed in a skin but also as a body in movement. I learn that my extension in space is differentiated and that my body has a mobile *form*. Suspended motionless in a warm bath, I feel merely comfortable. To realize clearly that I have toes, I must twiddle them. Other movements make me aware of having arms, legs, a neck, a spine, and so on.

Harwood's daughter (see page 23) said she wanted to see her father's watch by touching it. But to be in a fully dynamic relationship with the watch, she would have had to grasp it. In grasping something, we make use of our sense of touch (to feel its otherness), somatic sense (to feel its weightiness), and kinesthetic sense (to feel its shape). When we grasp a thought we mean that we are in a concrete relationship to it, as if the thought were a material object. After all, speaking etymologically, to comprehend means to understand by grasping.

The sense of movement is important for the development of our concept of space; as with the somatic sense, it is self-centered. Through movement, I come to know my own movement space, but not yet the space in which other bodies can move. I know only my own somatic territory. Geometrically, I would have to represent it with polar coordinates, radiating from my own center of awareness, extending to the limits of the movements of my arms and legs. The way in which this sense enables us to be aware of outer movement will be discussed later, when we examine the action of the eyes.

The Sense of Balance

This sense joins the sense of touch in bringing awareness of the surrounding world. Touch tells me that other

surfaces exist. Balance tells me that other *forces* exist. Just
as recognition of my skin and some other surface is inextricably coupled through the experience of touching, so is
the realization that there are forces in space coupled with
the experience of balancing my body. Balance is activated
by gravity, the force that tends to cause us to fall down. To
stand upright we must exert ourselves to overcome gravity
and maintain our balance. It is something we learn to do
as children. Through the sense of touch I become aware
of the solidity of the ground that supports me; through
the somatic sense I am aware of the effort needed to stand
upright. The movements required to stand up are conveyed by the kinesthetic sense. But it is the sense of balance that enables me to orient my body in space.

It is significant that the sense organ of balance consists of
three semicircular canals in the ear arranged at right
angles to one another. Working together, these canals
make it possible for us not only to orient ourselves in three
dimensions but also to perceive and think through the
concept of a three-dimensional space that is "public"—that
is, a space where forces and bodies other than ourselves
can exist and move. Our awareness of such a space grew
out of our need to constantly balance ourselves against the
"outside force" of gravity at work in this space.

In infants, the senses of movement and balance awaken
and become active from the head downward. A baby can
balance its head on its shoulders before being able to
stand upright. A baby sits before walking. The first steps of
the toddler are often accompanied by a broad smile: the
first triumph of the practical physicist, the craftsman, in
the physical world. Having become a master manipulator
of his or her own physical body, the child is then ready to
begin more extensive explorations of the surrounding

physical world. Children's skills in manipulating their own portion of the physical world, their body, are still far ahead of their capacity to manipulate the surrounding world; and their ability to conceptualize these skills into the abstract ideas of mass, movement, space, and energy will not awaken for some years. For now the applied physicist is at work, more or less unconsciously, slowly extending his or her experiments into the surrounding world. The scholar, however, is still asleep.

So we may sum up: The four modes of sense perception that enable us to directly perceive our own bodies are also the source for the essential ingredients of our materialistic picture of the world. This world contains no color, smell, sound, or warmth, but only movements of objects in space. The sense of touch allows me to say I have a surface. The somatic sense allows me to say I am a body with volume and mass. The sense of movement allows me to say I am a moving body with a mobile form. The sense of balance allows me to say I am a body moving in a space shared with other moving bodies.

The Body Reaches Out: Eyes

Let us now consider the complex mode of sense perception called seeing. Sight tends to dominate our language and our ways of imagining the activity of science. The "detached observer" is someone who is looking at the world—we do not speak of a detached *scenter* or *taster.* Although a strong stimulus to any of our senses could awaken us from sleep, we generally associate the process with the opening of our eyes when we begin to perceive our surroundings as a scene. This scene appears to us to be a public three-dimensional space in which moveable solid objects are located. Because it is so easy to believe that the materialistic outlook is based on seeing and not, as we have been arguing, on the "body-centered" senses, we must now examine the sense of sight with particular care.

We generally think of the eye as a kind of camera. But it is also a kind of limb, swivelled by muscles in the eye socket. Not only do we receive images from the world, but we also use our eyes as we would a limb, to "reach out" and investigate our surroundings. That this is so is indicated by the way in which human beings adapt to blindness, using arms and fingers for "seeing." There are many accounts of blind people who, upon first gaining sight through laser surgery, are still unable to see an object such as a tree even though they are looking directly at it. Such newly sighted individuals must first touch the tree and put their arms around it in order to actually see it. By touching it they are able to associate the set of relationships that form their concept *tree* with their newly gained visual capability. Only as the concept is augmented to incorporate visual aspects are they actually able to see the tree.

The blind are deprived of three important components of vision: shades of light and dark, color, and distance. The last mentioned, distance, is especially significant for the perception of form, which can otherwise be made up for by the sense of touch. The "horizon" shrinks to the limits of an outstretched limb or white stick. Nevertheless, hearing contributes much to our experience of depth and can replace, although without the precision, much of what is lost from the spatial aspect of vision. In sum, the only modes of sense experience of which a blind person is completely deprived are color and shades of light and dark.

The eye, when acting as a limb, is closely connected with the body-centered senses. Indeed, it serves as a kind of extension for them. When the eye is focused on an object, very fine scanning movements cause the image to move back and forth across the retina, an area of light-sensitive skin within the eyeball. Experiments that allow an image to be projected onto the retina and fixed in place have shown that the observer soon becomes blind; the image can no longer be seen. The illumination of the light-sensitive rods and cones must constantly be changing to make sight possible. If there is no change, the rods and cones soon cease to signal anything. This is true in an analogous way for the sense of touch. We are usually unaware of our clothes touching our skin until we shift position. We rub or stroke the texture of a surface, to "sense" it. Similarly, the eye jiggles the retinal image across the retina to achieve a kind of refined "touching."

The roles played by movement and balance in seeing are also well established. Just as a blind man wishing to apprehend the shape of an object moves his hands over it, so too, in seeing a shape, we do much more than simply look at it. We actually feel our way around the form with our eyes. Techniques have been developed that reveal the scanning movements involved. These movements are quite distinct and much larger in scale than the tiny jiggling movements used by the eye to "touch."

The function of the kinesthetic sense is much more difficult to understand; it seems so obvious that we observe movements "out there." Actually, the situation is much more complex. There are two ways to see movement in the surrounding world. The first is perception of systematic change of the retinal image. If we fixate a point on the horizon and then a bird flies across the field of vision, we see that the bird is moving. This is equivalent to the "movement" we would sense if a pencil is drawn along the skin of

our hand. The movement is inferred from a connected
series of touch experiences.

The second way of seeing movement uses the kinesthetic
sense proper. This sense is in play whenever we move our
eyes while keeping them focused on a moving object. In
this case we see a moving object against a steady background despite the fact that both the image of the moving
object and the image of the background are moving across
the retina. Since all of the images are moving, it cannot be
the motion across the retina that gives us the experience of
movement against a steady background. It is the kinesthetic sense unconsciously at work in the muscles of our
eyes that allows us to perceive the movements of our "eyeball limbs." Seeing movement is actually a very complex
act of data processing: directed movements of the muscles
in the eyes are combined with movements in the rest of the
body and then compared with the changes in the retinal
image. We see change immediately, but we see movement
in the surroundings only because of our (largely unconscious) knowledge of our own bodily movements, especially the movements of our eyeballs.

If movement in the world is not something that we simply
observe but are able to perceive only because of the sensations on the skin of the retina—"reading," so to speak, the
messages from the musculature of our own bodies, including the eyeballs—then the same must also be true for other
apparently familiar experiences of the world "out there." A
well-functioning sense of balance is also active in the sense
of sight. Look at a scene, then tilt your head abruptly. For a
brief moment it will appear that the world out there is rotat-
ing. When your head comes to rest, it seems the world
comes to rest too. Even if your head comes to rest tilted at
an angle to the horizon, the world will still appear right side

up despite its apparent rotation. Here again we do not simply "see" what is happening on the retina. Our perception of what is happening in the surrounding world is augmented by our sense of balance, which informs us of our own changing orientation to the vertical.

The fact that we use the word "surrounding" points to a world containing more than just movement and orientation. Our somatic sensations working together with the sense of movement convey to us a sense of volume of our bodies and thereby enable us to experience a "surrounding space" that has extension, volume, and depth.

Binocular vision is another aspect of seeing that is far more complex than we normally realize. The world seen through one eye lacks real depth. As is well known, we "see" depth by comparing two different retinal images. We also change the shape of the lenses of our eyes, by muscular effort, to bring into focus scenes at different distances. Here again, the eyes are working as limbs. Something similar to this occurs when a blind man, for example, explores depth and distance with movements of his limbs: the direct experience of bulk or extension in space is most vivid when we feel around an object and become aware of the distance between our hands. Such an apprehension for bulk is, of course, also mediated in part by the sense of movement. Yet an awareness of the volume of our own bodies as a basis of comparison (always in the background) seems to flow into all experience of volume. An illustration of this phenomenon is the odd feeling of walking behind an apparently solid tree on a stage set and discovering it to be only a surface. This example shows that we project into our surroundings a presumption of volume, bulk, solidity, and mass. These qualities are imagined into the world based upon largely unconscious concepts given us by senses located in our own bodies.

Thus we see that the eye is not only a camera, passively observing the world out there, it is also at work as a limb, reaching out into the surroundings. Our awareness of what this limb experiences is derived, as with other limbs, from the body-centered senses: touch, movement, balance, and the somatic sense. What the eyes convey through their camera-like function—namely, shades of light and dark and color—is of no importance for the materialistic worldview.

Earlier we noted (on page 18) the tendency of scientists to replace dynamic formulations of mechanics with kinematic ones; that is, to replace descriptions that include forces with ones purely in terms of observations. But to recognize that visual perception of objects moving in space *is* an act of participation in the world is to realize that there is no such thing as a mere observation. Consequently, the program of replacing dynamics with kinematics, while it is perhaps valid for utilitarian reasons and even for reasons of a conceptual nature, is nevertheless futile with regard to gaining a description independent of human involvement.

Galileo: Scholar and Craftsman

We have described scientific materialism as the offspring of two kinds of human activity: the work of the scholar and that of the craftsman. The first developed confident manipulation of thought, the second, manipulation of matter. But until the emergence of science in the fifteenth century, scholars had not paid much attention to matter, while craftsmen had yet to penetrate their know-how with clear concepts.

A critical aspect of what then happened is made visible in Galileo's *Assayer:*

Now I say that whenever I conceive of any material or corporeal substance, I immediately feel the need to think of it as bounded, as having this or that shape; as being large or small in relation to other things, and in some specific place at any given time; as being in motion or at rest; as touching or not touching some other body; as being one in number or few or many. From these conditions I cannot separate such a substance by any stretch of my imagination. But that it must be white or red, bitter or sweet, noisy or silent, or of sweet or foul odor, my mind does not feel compelled to bring in as necessary accompaniments. Without the senses as our guides, reason or imagination unaided would probably never arrive at qualities like these. Hence I think that tastes, odors, colors and so on are no more than mere names so far as the objects in which we place them are concerned, and that they reside only in the consciousness.... To excite in us tastes, odors and sounds I believe that nothing is required in external bodies except shapes, numbers and slow or rapid movements. [Drake 1957]

Thus, at the beginning of classical science Galileo limited his attention to a specific set of qualities: size, shape, quantity, and motion. Having given a few examples of how such qualities could produce personal reactions having nothing to do with the external, he tries to be more explicit about the cause of our experience of heat:

Those materials which produce heat in us and make us feel warmth, which are known by the general name of "fire," would then be a multitude of minute particles having certain shapes and moving with certain velocities. Meeting with our bodies they penetrate by means of their extreme subtlety, and their touch as felt by us when they pass through our substance is the sensation we call "heat." This is pleasant or unpleasant according to the greater or smaller speed of these particles as they go pricking and penetrating. [Drake 1957]

Galileo begins by building a picture of the "world outside" made up of imaginary solid bodies, the motion of which can be followed by kinematics and dynamics. He was not the only one to attempt such an explanation. In the second book of his *Novum Organum* (1620), Francis Bacon described the nature of heat in a very similar way. At the end of the seventeenth century the distinction between so-called primary qualities—for example, size, shape, number, and motion—and secondary qualities—such as taste, smell, sound, and color—was consolidated by John Locke in his *Essay Concerning Human Understanding*. Locke also maintained that the qualities of objects in the outer world produce ideas in our mind by sending out particles that interact with the human organism:

If then external objects be not united to our minds when they produce ideas therein, and yet we perceive these original qualities in such of them as singly fall under our senses, it is evident that some motion must be thence continued by our nerves, or animal spirits, by some parts of our bodies, to the brains or the seat of sensation, there to produce in our minds the particular ideas we have of them. And since the extension, figure, number, and motion of bodies of an observable bigness, may be perceived at a distance by sight, it is evident some singly imperceptible bodies must come from them to the eyes, and thereby convey to the brain some motion; which produces these ideals which we have of them in us. [Locke 1689]

This way of thinking was in the air in the seventeenth and early eighteenth centuries, and constituted "corpuscular philosophy."

Why then did science choose the body senses as a basis for conceptualizing the material world? The answer is usually advanced today that primary qualities are measurable, while secondary ones are not. However, it is striking that none of the corpuscular philosophers ever gave any reason for thinking as they did, except to mention that they felt compelled to do so or that it was evidently so. Apparently this way of thinking was intrinsic to the soul condition that developed naturally from the fifteenth century onward. Science emerged as part of a profound and revolutionary search for individual independence and freedom. The Reformation and the Renaissance are imbued with this mood in social life, the arts, religion, and in the worldwide voyages of exploration. In all these spheres, freedom presupposes that individuals can find certainty within, that they can, to some extent, control their surroundings and achieve their own insights. In prescientific cultures, certainty came from without, from hierarchical authorities, whether spiritual or secular. The conviction that individuals can and must find certainty for themselves, through a personal search for insight, was revolutionary, even heretical. Yet they did not have to search in a vacuum. They took hold of two threads of experience, the scholarly and the craft traditions, and wove them together. In this way, two old paths to certainty were transmuted into one new way.

The scholarly tradition included mathematics, which developed in large measure because of astronomy and the study of the heavens. For Pythagoras, mathematical thought embodied spiritual truths in an abstract form. Throughout the Middle Ages there was a similar preoccupation with the conceptualization of religious experience using Greek philosophical ideas. This feeling that pure thought, especially mathematical thought, was a reflection of spiritual truths, persisted in the early development of science. Copernicus and even Galileo, while using mathematics with ever increasing skill and confidence, nevertheless held to the conviction that the movements of the planets must be circular, since the circle is the form that embodies the perfection of the heavenly worlds.

Meanwhile, men from the craft traditions were beginning to use mathematics for their work. Leonardo da Vinci, the great artist-craftsman who was deeply concerned with "bodies" of all kinds, wrote: "There is no certainty in science where one of the mathematical sciences cannot be applied." Not long after, in the early sixteenth century, Italian engineer Niccolò Tartaglia regarded mathematics simply as a tool for terrestrial operations and published translations of Euclid's geometry and Archimedes' mechanics; he wrote: "The purpose of the geometrical student is always to make things that he can construct in material to the best of his ability."

When mathematics was abstracted from the heavens, so to speak, and began to be used as a means of illuminating the laws at work in matter, it joined with another kind of certainty: the confidence of the craftsman's know-how. But this confidence belongs, in a sense, to every human being. We all start life acquiring the know-how to manipulate our own physical body. When we have learned to walk, we have mastered, unconsciously, that portion of the physical world which supports us throughout life. From this mastery we derive both independence and confidence for our further explorations of the world.

Classical science was born when human beings began to experience themselves as isolated, largely independent of an alien "world out there." This condition arose between the fourteenth and seventeenth centuries. The philosophical and mathematical way of thinking of the scholars met and united with the "way of knowing" of the body senses on which the expertise of the craftsmen had largely been based. This meeting and union occurred in the world "in here." At the same time the world "out there" was being "explained" by an imaginary world of corpuscles. But these corpuscles were merely an externalization of the newly created "world in here." Measuring was introduced to establish a bridge between the mathematics of the scholar and the practical world of the craftsman. For classical scientists, measurement became the foundation of their confidence that their mathematics was dealing with the solid "world out there."

However, the model for even the most scientifically advanced measurement is the measurement of length using some kind of linear scale. When measuring length, the human observer determines a matchup between scale divisions and marks on the object to be measured. Thus, whoever measures uses only the most primitive of body senses. Using the eye as a limb, the direction of view is determined by some mark—for example, the end of the table to be measured—and the sense of movement in the eye is used to determine the scale division of the ruler nearest to the mark. If we want to measure qualities such as temperature, where this procedure is not possible, we have temperature produce changes in lengths of a liquid column or changes in electrical voltages or changes in the pressure of a gas, all of which can be measured directly or indirectly by scale or pointer readings.

Thus, the observer's activity when measuring is even more restricted than in any other aspect of classical science. At the same time, the actual change in the quality that produced the effect we are measuring is usually far removed from our scale or pointer readings. The measurement that produces the numbers needed to establish mathematical relationships is not fundamentally different from the other activities in classical science: Using the simplest body senses possible, we look at phenomena (meter readings, and so on), which give us food for mathematics, even though the phenomena actually observed are often only tenuously connected with what we are trying to understand. Measuring is, therefore, no guarantee that we have established a relationship between the two worlds, the one "in here" and the one "out there." This is only emphasized by modern measurements in which the observer is replaced wherever possible by electronic devices; the connections between the actual events that move the measuring instruments and the qualities we purport to be measuring are increasingly theoretical.

In the next chapter we shall show how classical science developed into modern science. The very new modes of thinking required by modern science make it possible for all the faculties of the human being to be involved in the development of science. Only such total involvement can guarantee that we have bridged the gap between the world "in here" and the world "out there."

3 . Changing Relations to Physical Reality

Having described the psychological and physiological origins of classical science, we shall now trace it historically, paying special attention to its evolution into modern science at the turn of the century. With classical scientists confining themselves to the use of four body senses, it is not surprising that the content of what actually has been observed has become increasingly restricted with the passage of time. Concurrently, the power of mathematics has been increasing. Observation and thinking have separated. Modern scientists have learned to think in ways that contradict ordinary experience. For example, according to modern theories solid bodies change shape and size when moving; also, events that are observed as being simultaneous by one person are not simultaneous for another. While early classical scientists sought to fathom God's thoughts when he created the universe, modern scientists doubt whether science leads to any truth at all. They wonder whether they are not limited to constructing "models" (the word "model" will be defined later) useful for controlling limited parts of nature. We shall attempt to demonstrate that the separation of observation from thinking and the use of mathematics in general are achievements of permanent value. We believe them to represent the single most significant step in the development of human consciousness since the Middle Ages. Our story again begins with Galileo.

The Origins of Terrestrial and Celestial Mechanics

Galileo was exceptionally versatile; he was the epitome of a Renaissance man. An accomplished musician and writer, he chose not to write in Latin but in the vernacular, using his native Italian with proficiency, charm, and wit. Those who became the objects of his often biting irony were hardly ever skilled enough as writers to retaliate in kind, a fact that accounts, in part, for Galileo's many implacable enemies. Because he was both a charming artist and an innovative thinker, he gained access to those in power. A valued servant of the Venetian government and of the dukes of Tuscany, he was also for many years a welcome visitor to the papal court in Rome. Only with the greatest reluctance did the Church finally decide to discipline him. This polished courtier also moved freely among artisans in the arsenals and shipyards of Venice, and his scientific work owed much to what he learned from artisans. A skilled craftsman himself, he fashioned with his own hands telescopes and geometrical instruments of his own design. In his scientific work Galileo was both an inventive experimenter and a penetrating theoretician. We shall see how he combined the experience of the craftsman with the thinking of the scholar through a description of his investigations in mechanics.

Some of the reasons he came into conflict with the Church will also become apparent.

There is a well-known story about the way Galileo is supposed to have made one of his major discoveries. Sitting in the cathedral at Pisa, he noticed the lamps swinging in front of the altar. Using his pulse to time them, he found the length of time required for the swing of each lamp to be independent of the extent of the sweep. The time for one swing seemed to depend only on the length of the suspension. This was a surprising discovery: one might have expected a pendulum to take longer for a sweep two feet wide than for a sweep of one foot. Galileo found, as near as he could tell, that the two times were the same. His later experimentation with pendulums not only confirmed the constancy of the time of the swing but also revealed that a pendulum, when arriving at the end of its sweep, very nearly reaches the same height from which it started. This is so even if the length of suspension is shortened during the swing. In the following diagram, a pendulum starting at *A* swings to *B*, where *AB* is very nearly a horizontal line. If a peg is fixed at *P*, so that the suspension is effectively shortened in midswing, the pendulum swings to *C*, where *AC* is again very nearly a horizontal line. Galileo surmised that in the ideal case, with no air resistance or friction, the pendulum, once started, would go on swinging indefinitely from *A* to *B* and back again to *A*, or from *A* to *C* and back again to *A*.

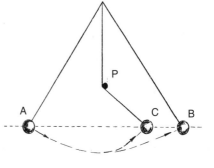

The last thought may appear obvious and simple to us now. This was not so in Galileo's time, when thinking about the sense world was much more bound up with perception than it is now. Air resistance, friction, and similar forces were experienced as part and parcel of the world and could not simply be thought away. The works of Aristotle and innumerable commentaries on them (the standard textbooks of physics at the time) contained, for example, many proofs to show that a vacuum cannot exist, that nature abhors a vacuum. The picture of reality came from the experience of those working in the crafts, who may have tried to reduce friction to make their work easier but never imagined it could be eliminated completely. The technological know-how of the time included an instinctive appreciation of the world as it is with all its complexities, including friction, resistance, ropes that stretch, and bodies that deform. Moreover, the cause of anything that happened in the world was imagined in a manner similar to the way a craftsman might have caused it. An effort always had to be made to bring about a change in the surroundings. Hence, if no one could be identified who brought about the change, it was natural to assume that some other agency actively working in a similar fashion was responsible. At that time, for example, the planets were pictured as being moved by otherworldly intelligences.

Unchanging perfection, on the other hand, belonged to quite a different world, the world of Plato's perfect, eternal ideas, a world familiar to the scholar. Mathematics, according to Plato, lay somewhere between the world of perfect, immutable ideas and the sense world, where change holds sway. Aristotle emphasized that the mathematical laws that he applied to the motion of the planets were only there for calculating observed paths; the spheres he postulated were not necessarily real. His geometrical constructions had, he felt, fulfilled their purpose when they had predicted a conjunction between Jupiter and Mars in the constellation Leo on a certain night. The construction was a good one if, on looking in the direction of Leo on the night in question, Mars and Jupiter were in fact observed very close to each other. The actual causes of the motion of the planets were hierarchically arranged forces that began with the prime mover at the periphery of the universe. The prime mover, at least, if not the planetary orbs, had to be endowed with soul to bring about the motion of the planets. In the Middle Ages the planets were moved by the souls of the intelligences, identified by some as the Christian hierarchies, that is, the angels, archangels, and others, who carried out the will of God. These hierarchies were considered the divine model for the hierarchies of the Church, which, in turn, carried out the will of God on Earth.

Galileo broke radically with the Aristotelian tradition when he imagined a pendulum swinging in a vacuum without friction, following exactly the mathematical laws used for constructing its path. Moreover, he insisted that the mathematical laws discovered by Copernicus were actual realities. Copernicus himself had described them as an alternative to the Ptolemaic constructions, which had in their turn replaced those of Eudoxus used by Aristotle. He did not publicly claim any more reality for his circles and epicycles, with the Sun at the center, than for those of Ptolemy, with the Earth at their center. The Church had no objection to a new mathematical model and suggested to Galileo that he follow the example of Copernicus. But Galileo insisted that the Sun was at the center i*n reality*. This claim upset the whole structure of the hierarchies surrounding the Earth and implicitly undermined the authority of the Church, which was modeled on that structure. Church fathers were afraid Galileo's new ideas would endanger the stable fabric of society, a fabric already weakened by the Reformation. In the eyes of the Church no crime was committed by using Copernicus's heliocentric system as a mathematical hypothesis. What was deeply disturbing, if not heretical, was Galileo's insistence that a mathematical hypothesis worked out by a scholar could and did describe accurately the reality created by the Divine Craftsman.

Galileo's experiments with falling bodies illustrate another important aspect of the new thinking. Since free-falling bodies descend too fast to be timed accurately, he had the brilliant idea of using spheres rolling down inclined planes instead. He suspected that the cause of the downward motion and the mathematical laws governing it would be the same in both cases. Here we have another example of the type of thinking mentioned earlier: despite all real and obvious differences, Galileo surmised that the governing laws would be the same for the descent of objects in free fall and along inclined planes. Experimenting with spheres rolling down inclined planes, he verified his expectations regarding falling bodies: when falling freely in a vacuum they would accelerate uniformly (that is, increase velocity by the same amount every second) and the rate of acceleration would not depend upon the weight of the body.

The work with inclined planes was combined with his study of the pendulum to produce another very important idea: bodies left to themselves would continue moving indefinitely if there were no friction or air resistance.

It is intriguing to see how he made this idea clear to others. He imagined a sphere S (see diagram) rolling down the plane AB and then rolling up one of the planes BC, BD, BE. Following the clue of the pendulum's motion, Galileo assumed that the sphere would reach the points F, G, H at the height at which it started. To make this assumption, one must not only think away friction and air resistance, one must also neglect the impact of the sphere on the second plane at B. After thinking about the problem in this extremely abstract way, Galileo asked what would happen if the second plane were level, as is BK. This question led easily to the idea that the sphere would go on rolling forever and foreshadowed the concept of inertia.

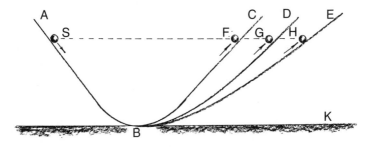

Galileo went on to ask what would happen if BK were a table, K being its edge. The sphere would then follow a parabolic trajectory to the ground as the result of having two independent motions: one never ending and horizontal combined with one uniformly accelerated and vertical. This was also verified by experiment.

While Galileo investigated the motion of heavy bodies near Earth using a combination of physical and thought experiments with comparatively simple mathematics, Kepler produced a completely new picture of the motion of the planets by applying much more complicated mathematics to Tycho Brahe's excellent observations of the motions of the planets, particularly those of the planet Mars. It is interesting that Kepler was motivated in his herculean mathematical labors by the search for a Pythagorean harmony among the planets, in fact, by a search for the harmony of the spheres. Kepler's kinematical laws, the laws for which he is now famous, are well hidden in his books; for him they were auxiliary discoveries. Since these are the laws later used by Newton for constructing his dynamic "System of the World," we shall remind the reader of them:

1. A planet moves in an ellipse with the Sun as one of its foci.
2. The line joining the planet to the Sun sweeps out equal areas in equal times.
3. The cube of the semimajor axis of the ellipse is proportional to the square of the period of revolution of the planet.

Just as Galileo describes the paths of the projectiles near the Earth by mathematically specifying how their velocities change, so Kepler defines mathematically the path of each planet, specifying how its velocity changes, and, in the third law, provides a mathematical relationship between the orbits of all the planets belonging to the same system. These laws are kinematical in that they only describe motion without alluding to forces causing them.

We can now take up the work of Isaac Newton. He defined mathematically the notions of mass and force, relating them to the acceleration of moving bodies. He made it possible to calculate the effects of such forces as friction and air resistance so that the actual, not just theoretical, trajectories of projectiles could be calculated. In Newton's picture, forces were exerted by bodies impinging on each other or pushing and pulling each other through ropes, shafts, gears, and so on. These forces were imagined much like those exerted by human beings and animals. Where no perceptible living or inanimate force-producing agency could be identified, yet bodies in motion continued to accelerate, some other force had to be postulated: "Universal Gravitation." This is the force that we experience as the weight of bodies and that propelled the proverbial apple onto Newton's head. However, it was supposed to act between any two material bodies. For instance, gravity was pictured as acting between the Sun and the planets and between the planets themselves. It was difficult to understand how inert objects could exert forces on each other across vast, interplanetary distances with no perceptible connection, and Newton was accused of introducing occult agencies into nature. Nevertheless, he developed simple mathematical laws for gravitation, enabling him to show that gravity could both keep planets moving according to Kepler's laws and make bodies near the Earth move as Galileo described. In this way Newton unified terrestrial and celestial mechanics.

Newton's scheme was immensely successful. The telescopes perfected by the astronomers of the eighteenth and nineteenth centuries made possible astronomical discoveries that fitted perfectly into the mathematical-mechanical picture. Galileo and Kepler used mathematics simply to describe the motion of bodies in terms of positions, paths, velocities, and accelerations. Newton's inclusion of force into this picture completed the penetration of body-sense experience by the thought of the scholar.

The Lonely Self

How does a human being on Earth experience the universe? Individuals are no longer protectively surrounded by divinity as they were in the medieval universe. Humans now see themselves racing through space on a small speck of matter, the Earth, which is prevented by only a tenuous attachment to the Sun from losing its way into empty space. Human beings can no longer look outside for guidance. They must find security and guidance from within. Following the development of religion and philosophy, we see that humanity was being prepared for this experience from the fifteenth century onward. Jan Hus, Martin Luther, Zwingli, and others had found their own individual connections to God independently of the Church. Protestants were learning to rely on their consciences and their own interpretations of the Bible. They felt they no longer needed the mediation or the protection of the Church's hierarchies to reach God. The inner life of the human being was increasingly prepared to rely on itself, while the immediate vicinity, so to speak, around each person was emptied of the Divine. George Fox discovered a living "Inner Light" while the outer light became dead and mechanical. God appeared inside the human soul or was relegated to an abstract heaven very far away.

However, the inner light of the personality was not always kindled by Divine Light. Descartes bore witness to the way in which a person can feel cut off from the world and full of doubt. With thoughts similar to those expressed by Galileo in *The Assayer,* he had no confidence in the pictures presented by the senses. Although at the start his thought seemed to give some certainty, he then mused, "What if there were an evil deceiver active in my soul who arranged my thoughts so as to lead me astray?" Descartes seemed to experience that thoughts came into his mind from somewhere unknown, just as the senses conjure up colors, sounds, smells, and tastes out of an unknown world "out there." Anything could exist in that world outside his consciousness, not only a good God but also an evil deceiver. He asked whether there was anything inside his private world, the "world in here," about which he could be certain. He described how he suddenly found such an experience: He was certain of the inner activity of his doubting. His famous saying "I think, therefore I am" should really read "I doubt, therefore I am." Descartes found a firm foundation for cognition in his experience of inner activity, an activity he realized took place entirely within himself.

Both Descartes and Newton used mostly mathematics to construct their pictures of the "world out there." We find that the early practitioners of classical science were isolated individuals with firm confidence in their own mathematical thinking. They also believed firmly in a mechanical world of inanimate matter composed of moving solid bodies or vortices outside themselves. The origin of the "corpuscular philosophy" espoused by seventeenth- and eighteenth-century "natural philosophers" is now clear. Although they would not deny their experiences of colors, sounds, and all the other secondary qualities, nevertheless, for these scientists solid bodies moving in space were preeminently real because such bodies could be dealt with reliably using their thinking. That is why Galileo pondered how moving particles could cause the sensation of heat. Newton applied very similar thinking to light and expressed the results in one of the queries attached to his *Optics*: "Are not the rays of light very small bodies emitted from shining substances?" In many ways they and their contemporaries were responsible for populating the whole of the "world out there" with their imagined mechanisms. They imagined how particles would have to behave, what properties they would need, in order to produce the sensations of heat and light. Further developed and refined, corpuscular philosophy became the kinetic theory of heat and the atomic theory of chemistry in the nineteenth century. According to this theory, one would agree with another of the suggestions Newton placed at the end of his *Optics*:

> It seems probable to me, that God in the beginning formed matter in solid, massy, hard, impenetrable, moveable particles, of such sizes and figures, and with such other properties, and in such proportion to space, as most conduced to the end for which he formed them; even so very hard, as never to wear or break into pieces.

Nineteenth-century chemists were convinced that atoms were neither created nor destroyed in any chemical reaction; this fact is expressed in the law of conservation of matter. They were also convinced that atoms of one element never changed into atoms of another.

We have seen that a great change in the way human beings experience reality occurred in the centuries between the Middle Ages and the seventeenth century. While medieval humanity looked into the world to understand itself, seventeenth-century humanity looked into itself to understand the world. The individual became isolated from the world. In the imagination of the scientist, the outer world changed from a living, sprouting, warm, and colorful home into a bowling alley for dead, solid, small particles of varying shapes, masses, and sizes. This was the only view that could be described by mathematics and therefore experienced with the self-evident certainty of the thinking mind. Hence, Galileo was confident that the reality of his experience was self-evident. As a consequence, new technology was discovered that changed the outer world not only in imagination but also in reality.

The Rise of Technology and the Concept of Energy

Technology has, of course, existed since the time of the Pharaohs. We can admire the skill of the goldsmiths, enamelers, and glassworkers as well as the power of the pyramid builders. Improvements in the trades were certainly made from time to time. However, the rate of technological change since Galileo has been so great that modern technology cannot be compared to anything that existed previously. Why did the isolation of the individual from the environment bring about such a dramatic spurt in technological development?

We find the answer to this question if we compare the activity of the craftsman with that of the "natural philosopher" of the seventeenth century. The craftsman is intimately connected with his work. He may experience while hammering how a change in direction of the blows makes the work easier, and he might invent a new form of support for the work. While assembling a structure, he might see how an additional member could increase the strength. New inventions and improvements came about because the craftsman was dealing directly with his work. Contemplating the piece while in bed at night, he imagined how the working conditions or the product could be improved.

New science practitioners worked quite differently. Having learned to derive general principles and to picture idealized situations that never occur in reality, they were able to manipulate these principles and pictures in the privacy of their isolated minds where there were no constraints to inhibit changes. They were much freer than the craftsman to imagine new possibilities and new arrangements of well-known forces. Although an invention can be constructed relatively easily in the mind, anyone who has tried it knows how long it usually takes to make it work in practice. Nevertheless, the ability of the human mind to work theoretically on problems opened up new and radically different methods of bringing about change in the world.

The machinery of the early industrial revolution, of the seventeenth and eighteenth centuries, driven by water and later by steam, was still designed and improved by craftsmen. However, in the nineteenth century, scientific principles were increasingly applied in technology. The method of idealization was used very fruitfully, for instance, by Sadi Carnot and his successors. Carnot imagined an ideal heat engine that could no more be realized in practice than could Galileo's frictionless inclined planes. Nevertheless, such an ideal engine provided an important design criterion. Furthermore, thinking about such ideal machines led to the development of new concepts. Perhaps the most important was the concept of energy, originally conceived in the effort to understand mechanical processes. Later it was used to describe how heat produced mechanical effects in steam engines and, conversely, how mechanical motion produced heat when opposed by friction. Gradually the somewhat elusive concept of energy, which could appear in the guises of heat, motion, light, or electricity, entered the scientific world-view. The rather complicated mathematical treatment of energy necessary for the design of heat engines and for understanding the new science of thermodynamics could be understood only by experts. Nevertheless, energy, made indestructible by the law of conservation of energy, entered the popular nineteenth-century picture of the world. In this world immutable atoms combined and separated, exchanging a limited and constant supply of energy in the process. It was a universe in which the future resulted from the present following the necessity of entirely mechanical laws. For the educated person of that time, this was how the world really was.

Electricity Challenges Mechanical Thinking

Newton's universe contained a dubious element—the force of gravity. Because no physical agent could be found for its action, gravity was neither imaginable nor directly perceptible. In the course of the seventeenth and eighteenth centuries, two other forces with very similar properties became increasingly familiar: electricity and magnetism. By the end of the eighteenth century, enough was known for them to enter the scientific world picture, which they revolutionized in the course of the next century. They also gave rise to new mathematical concepts not as obviously anthropomorphic as were the concepts of force, energy, and mass. The existence of electricity and magnetism was surmised in a way similar to the discovery of gravitation. Rubbed amber will set small pieces of straw or paper in motion without material linkage, while the iron ore magnetite does the same with iron bodies. Rubbed amber, however, does not move iron, while magnetite does not move straw or wool. There must be two separate agencies capable of exerting forces that can produce the observed accelerations in inert bodies without actually touching them.

Electricity and magnetism work in a realm of the world in which we are not at home with our senses. In the sense-perceptible world these agents produce forces, light and heat effects, and on occasion violent contraction of our muscles. However, we have no sense that can tell us directly whether a piece of iron is magnetized, whether a glass rod is electrified, or whether a wire carries an electric current. Scientists were thrown back on their imaginations and on analogies taken from the sense world when investigating these agents. In the seventeenth and eighteenth centuries there was much talk of electric and magnetic "effluvia," extremely tenuous kinds of vapors emitted and absorbed by electrified and magnetized bodies when they acted on their surroundings. These analogies did not lead to much progress in scientific understanding.

Progress started when it was postulated that electric charges and magnetic poles exert electric and magnetic forces on each other at a distance (that is, without material linkage) just as material bodies exert gravitational forces on each other. It was possible to establish for these forces mathematical laws having the same form as the law of gravitation. The only difference was that electric and magnetic forces would attract or repel according to the nature of the charges and poles, while gravitational forces always attracted.

The notion of electrified and magnetized bodies acting on each other at a distance was considered by many to be a serious flaw. Such criticism, already expressed concerning gravity, was based on the conviction that science had no place for "occult" existences requiring no perceivable means of action. The forces produced by electric charges and magnetic poles as well as by massive bodies seemed to lead to such an "occult" life. These criticisms were eliminated by the introduction of a new agent in the concept of a field of force. Michael Faraday first conceived of such a field of force in a form useful to science. He was helped in his conception by a mechanical analogy. He knew how a force is transmitted through an elastic medium, through the shaft of a carriage, for instance. Inside the material of the shaft there are stresses and strains while the pull is being applied, and the shaft increases slightly in length and decreases in diameter. Picturing such stresses and strains in empty space, Faraday imagined that an electrified or magnetized body modified the surrounding space, establishing a field of force in it, just as the pull establishes a field of stresses within a shaft. Far from eliminating "occult agents," Faraday introduced new ones: fields of force penetrating space, unobservable to our senses, but very real in their effects. Space was no longer just an empty container. Indifferent to its material content, it became potentially the carrier of forces. Einstein went further than Faraday, making space itself the carrier of gravitational fields. For him, space became active in its own right.

Because fields of force could be described mathematically in far greater detail than action at a distance, Faraday's picture proved much more fertile than Newton's. Using the mathematical apparatus developed in fluid mechanics, James Maxwell then worked out a mathematical theory for Faraday's field of force. He predicted that disturbances in the electric and magnetic fields would propagate in waves in just the same way as disturbances in an elastic medium. If an elastic medium, such as air, is set vibrating at some point, by the blowing of a flutist, for example, a sound wave travels through the air from the flute to the ear of the listener. Similarly, an electrical or magnetic disturbance starts a wave in empty space. After these electromagnetic waves were identified experimentally by Heinrich Hertz, they solved a problem that had appeared a few decades earlier. It had been very difficult to accommodate light within Newton's mechanical worldview. Close examination of shadows had revealed that edges never became perfectly sharp; parallel to the edges there always appeared narrow dark and light stripes. This phenomenon had not attracted much attention until the beginning of the nineteenth century. At that time it was discovered that a series of dark and light stripes (interference or diffraction patterns) are produced when two or more illuminations originating from the same source are superimposed. It was difficult to see how such stripes could be produced by Newton's explanation of light as a stream of particles. Many of these small-scale light and dark phenomena bore a remarkable resemblance to standing waves on the surface of a pond. Although they could be accounted for if light was pictured as a train of waves, no material medium could be visualized for carrying these waves. Compared with ordinary materials, all media proposed for carrying these waves had impossibly paradoxical properties.

This is where Maxwell came in, using his equations to calculate the expected velocity of electromagnetic waves. Since this turned out to be the same as the measured velocity of light, it was assumed that light was made up of electromagnetic waves. Hence it was unnecessary to find a material medium for carrying light waves; a new medium was postulated, the luminiferous ether, which needed electrical and magnetic but no material properties. Maxwell's mathematics applied to Faraday's discovery led to the recognition of a hitherto unknown entity in nature: electromagnetic waves. The wave theory of light could now be completed. Electromagnetic waves of very high frequencies were assumed to affect the eye, producing the sensation of sight. Electromagnetic waves of much lower frequencies—those found by Hertz—were soon used for sending signals without wire from England to Newfoundland.

Our entry into the realm of electricity and magnetism, in which our senses are deficient, was made possible through analogy and mathematics. No longer could scientists observe and then perform experiments in order to interpret observations conceptually. They used analogy and mathematics to surmise the nature of events under specified sets of conditions. Experiments served to test whether predictions were actually fulfilled. If the test was positive, it was further assumed that the surmise corresponded to some reality in the electric and magnetic realms. However, scientists were conscious of their thoughts only in the form of analogy—for example, "a charged *particle*," "a *stream* of electricity," "moving under electric *pressure*," and so on. Gradually the analogies were given the status of reality; by force of habit the previously "occult" acquired the status of physical reality. While we know that *some* of the aspects of electricity and magnetism have mathematical and functional similarities to stress and strain, fluid flow, particle motion, and so forth, and that these mechanical analogues enable us to control those aspects of electricity and magnetism, we actually have no idea whether there are other intrinsic aspects of this realm of which we know nothing. We usually know the two realms compared by analogy, but when finding analogies for electricity and magnetism we know only one of them.

The understanding of electricity and magnetism gained through employing mechanical analogies was then reflected back on the mechanical picture of the universe, modifying it significantly. The world picture of classical physics at the end of the nineteenth century contained three different entities. First, there was *matter*, which consisted of ninety-two different kinds of atoms. Neither created nor destroyed, atoms kept all their properties indefinitely. Second, there were *electromagnetic waves* of different frequencies. Certain frequency ranges were imagined as sense-perceptible light and heat. Finally, there was *energy*. Whether appearing as mechanical or electromagnetic energy, the total amount in the universe is fixed and definite.

To come to this nineteenth-century view, human beings relied increasingly on mathematics and imaginative faculties to create inner pictures that might be accurate representations of an outer reality. The ability to think in a mathematical fashion and to create imaginative pictures was developed in the "world in here." That is why today we feel such confidence in our mathematical models when triumphs of science seem to prove that they have something to do with the "world out there." The human ability to think and imagine independently of sense appearances joined with an increasing facility with mathematics to make the birth and further development of classical science possible. Beginning with Galileo's ideal representations of mechanics and continuing with Maxwell's conception of the dynamics of electricity and magnetism and beyond, the human mind's facility with images free from sense perception has been increasing even as classical physics was being superseded by modern science with its quantum and relativity theories. We turn next to that modern science.

The Enigma of Quantum Reality

The picture of a world of three-dimensional space, empty except for an immutable amount of energy apportioned between matter and electromagnetic radiation in ever-changing distributions, began to fall apart at the turn of the twentieth century. The initial discomfiture came from two sources. On the one hand, the mathematics supporting physics was inadequate to describe the exchange of energy between atoms and electromagnetic waves during emission and absorption processes. For example, following the mathematics of classical science, the hot coals of a fire should glow blue rather than the familiar red of our experience. Here, no new phenomena are involved, only a failure of theory. On the other hand, entirely new phenomena entered the world; one type of atom was discovered to change into another type, with energy apparently produced out of nothing. This was the completely unexpected experimental discovery of radioactivity. The immutability of matter and energy, usually expressed in the form of so-called conservation laws, was put into jeopardy. Furthermore, the radioactive rays were difficult to categorize either wholly as particles or as waves. Gamma rays, for example, penetrated matter very easily and were therefore difficult to think of as particles. Yet they initially showed very few properties characteristic of electromagnetic waves.

At the turn of the century Max Planck solved the puzzle of the color of hot coals by introducing discontinuities, called quanta, into the light-emitting process. Five years later Albert Einstein did something similar for the photoelectric effect. In the photoelectric effect, light is absorbed by matter instead of being emitted; certain metals lose negative charge when illuminated. This process became the basis of many familiar automatic devices activated by the interruption of a light beam. In order to gain a proper mathematical description of this effect, Einstein hypothesized, as did Planck, that the light was quantized. The light was treated not in the usual way, as a continuous wave, but instead as a succession of particles that bombarded the illuminated metal to "dislodge" the electrical charge.

The blurring of the absolute distinction between waves and particles, a distinction fundamental to classical science, had—and still has—far-reaching implications for understanding the nature of physical reality. Within quantum science it cannot be said that a wave is a wave or a particle a particle. Under some conditions a particular entity will behave as a wave, under others as a particle. This so-called wave-particle duality presents a paradox insoluble to ordinary thinking about physical reality. With this paradox we pay for having presumed to solve the paradox of action at a distance.

Einstein's deep sense of the harmony and unity of nature was greatly disturbed by this paradox. He illustrated the problem vividly by conceiving a situation in which light impinges on a semi-reflecting mirror—that is, a mirror that allows some light to be transmitted through it while at the same time reflecting some of it. If we place photographic film behind the mirror to detect any light passing through and another sheet of film in front to detect the reflected light, we think that any given photon must be recorded on only one of the two photographic plates. (A photon is the name given to a quantum of light, which Einstein pictured to be a particle.) The photon is either reflected from the mirror or transmitted through it. We can think of only one or the other possibility, not both of them. However, replacing the photographic plates with completely reflecting mirrors produces the previously mentioned interference phenomena, which could be created only by light waves being reflected from both mirrors at the same time. Einstein emphasized that in the first case light is either transmitted through or reflected by the semi-reflecting mirror, while in the second case it is both reflected and transmitted. Yet only the detecting equipment has changed. The basic apparatus producing the phenomenon is unchanged. We must think of the phenomenon in ways that appear mutually exclusive. Many of the differences between the occult quantum world of the subatomic and our "ordinary" world can be grasped through Einstein's example.

We see that it is ultimately not possible to picture subatomic entities as "things" or "objects" in the usual sense. Mental pictures based upon human sense experience are apparently not always appropriate when extended beyond the bounds of that experience. In the example given, the difficulties arise because we are asked to picture objects and processes that do not occur anywhere in the realm of human sense experience.

In Einstein's example, particle-like subatomic events are governed by probability mathematics. Whether or not a given photon will be reflected or transmitted at the mirror is completely unknown. However, some percentage of any given stream of photons, depending on the particular mirror, will be recorded on each photographic plate. Every photon has a definite probability of being either reflected or transmitted. This result has far-reaching consequences, for it replaces the usual cause-effect relationships of classical science with those that are predictable according to chance. It is this aspect of quantum mechanics that inspired Einstein's famous remark, "God does not play dice."

A further aspect of such experiments appears to be this: the detecting apparatus seems to determine the phenomenon observed. The use of photographic film as a light detector "actualizes" the particle aspect of light, while the use of mirrors "actualizes" the wave aspect. Thinking of light in this fashion raises a question: How does the light "know" whether it is being detected with photographic film or being actualized as a wave with mirrors, and then behave accordingly? Or is it the experimenter who decides which aspect of reality will be observed, by determining the design of the detecting apparatus? This train of thought leads to the question of whether it still can be maintained that the scientific observer is separate from the observed. Since the time of Descartes this separation has provided the basis for claiming that science as a way of knowing is objective. Do scientists participate in the phenomenon observed? Do they take part in it by actually producing a reality that accords with the chosen experimental setup?

Finally, and perhaps most importantly, quantum mechanical phenomena ask us to join together in our thinking mutually exclusive aspects of the same reality, for example, the opposites of wave and particle, continuity and discreteness, causality and chance.

Since Einstein proposed the example of the wave-particle duality at the beginning of this century, quantum mechanics has had extraordinary success in explaining and predicting the observed behavior of matter. Nevertheless, to this day quantum theory remains utterly inexplicable using the mental pictures that served classical physics. For this reason, it challenges us to develop a thinking not bound to the world of empirical experience.

Relativity Theory Also Challenges Ordinary Thinking

Unlike quantum mechanics, which grew out of the failure of classical theories of physics to account for ordinarily observed results, relativity theory had its seed in Einstein's experience of an aesthetic flaw in the classical electromagnetic theory developed by Maxwell. Einstein saw that the flaw could be removed by a fundamental rethinking of the classical treatment of space and time.

In order to get the flavor of relativity, imagine a train moving at a constant speed past a station. A juggler in the train and one on the platform would have to cope with exactly the same laws of mechanics. However, the balls of the juggler on the train would have different velocities than would the balls of the juggler on the platform, since they would have the additional velocity imparted by the train. This situation is similar to that of Galileo's imagined sphere that, after rolling off a table, would have two velocities—one horizontal and one vertical—that combine to produce a parabolic trajectory.

Most of the laws of physics observed in the train would be the same as those observed on the platform. Only the velocity of the train would have to be added by an observer on the platform in order to follow events in the train. This would apply also to sound emitted by a flute in the train. For an observer in the train, the sound would travel with the same velocity in all directions; for the platform observer the sound moving in the same direction as the train would travel faster than the sound moving in the opposite direction.

To eliminate the worrisome aesthetic flaw, Einstein assumed that what has just been described is true for everything except light and all electromagnetic waves. Light emitted by a bulb in the train would spread out with the same velocity in all directions for every observer, whether in the train or on the platform. Einstein seems to have realized that this assumption had to be made on theoretical grounds. Others, having different expectations, had tried to show experimentally that light waves in the luminiferous ether behaved similarly to sound waves in the air. They attempted to detect variations in the speed of light relative to an observer moving through the ether in which light waves were assumed to be propagated. Such experiments had always failed to detect any differences. Apparently the velocity of light is the same for all observers, however they are moving; that is, unlike the movements of physical bodies in the universe as we perceive it, the speed of light is not relative to any physical object. Einstein's assumption could also have been put forward as an experimental result. Again we see that electromagnetic waves do not fit in with the ordinary thinking of classical science.

It is important to bear in mind that Einstein discovered this anomalous behavior of light through thinking and not experimentally. Rethinking how the same events could appear differently to different observers, he found it necessary to start with a new assumption. This is how he arrived at new ways of thinking about the fundamental properties of space, time, and measurements. Some of the results produced by his theory seemed paradoxical in the light of classical physics. For instance, events simultaneous for one observer would not necessarily be simultaneous for others, and the length of an object would appear differently to different observers. However, these effects become significant only when the relative speeds between objects and observers approach that of light in a vacuum. The speed of light is not only independent of the velocity of the observer but is also the maximum speed for signals and for physical bodies. If we calculate the movements of ordinary bodies moving at "everyday" speeds using classical mechanics and then using relativity theory, the differences are so small as to be undetectable by our measuring instruments. Only particles produced naturally by radioactive substances and artificially in particle accelerators move fast enough for these differences to be detectable. Whenever the difference is significant, relativity mechanics yields results corresponding to actual measurements, while classical mechanics contradicts the experiment. Relativity mechanics applies to all possible velocities, that is, to all velocities less than the velocity of light in a vacuum, while Newtonian, or classical, mechanics is a perfectly adequate approximation for ordinary velocities.

There is another important feature distinguishing classical from relativity mechanics. According to the latter, the acceleration of a given body by a given force depends not only on the body and the force but also on the speed. The faster a body is moving, the more difficult is further acceleration. According to classical physics, acceleration depends only on force and mass, which measures a body's constant inertia. In relativity theory, the inertia of a body, along with the mass that measures it, are not constant but actually increase with velocity. Speaking loosely one can say that "energy has mass." Mathematical analysis predicts the famous equation $E = mc^2$, the equivalence of mass and energy, which is the basis for utilizing so-called "atomic energy."

We want to stress the fact that whenever we are concerned with ultrasmall dimensions, as in quantum mechanics, or ultralarge velocities, as in relativity theory, the only guide to thinking is mathematics. All the concepts come out of mathematics. We are led to new worlds only insofar as we can grasp them with mathematics, which also enables us to manipulate these new worlds. Every attempt to think about these worlds with ordinary mental pictures has failed.

Models and the Creation of Scientific Knowledge

Let us briefly retrace the path we have followed in order to better understand the present situation of science. How have scientists discovered the laws of nature in their mathematical form?

First of all, scientists made idealized mental pictures of the phenomena to be understood. Theoretical mechanics was born when heavy, pointlike particles, perfectly rigid bodies sliding on frictionless planes, ideally circular wheels turning on absolutely smooth axles being pulled by weightless ropes, and so on, became the objects of mathematical thinking. These were models directly perceptible to the mind representing human experience "out there." The mathematics was then applied to increasingly nonideal situations, such as friction and deformation, and the weights of the agents pulling or pushing were gradually introduced into the idealized situations as well. The practical solutions were built up from solutions to many smaller problems, each one involving some different aspect of mechanics. The simplest results were purely kinematic. The introduction of mass and force led to dynamics.

Gravity, electricity, and magnetism required the introduction of the concept of imperceptible fields of force. The mathematics for this new field was, to start with, developed by analogy to elasticity and fluid flow. However, the mathematics of fields soon established itself as a discipline independent of the analogies that brought it to birth. The imperceptible (occult or supersensible) fields became respectable citizens of the scientific world. Similarly, energy, a chameleon-like disembodied entity that could appear in many different guises, was accepted as a bona fide entity, of which, at the beginning of time, God had created a definite amount. Energy could be transmitted from one place to another by moving masses, by waves in elastic media, or by fields of force.

Until the advent of the atomic model of matter, scientists had developed mathematical ideas in an almost instinctive interplay between observation and thought. This was not true of the next model, which "explained" the differences between solids, liquids, and gases in terms of the motion of atoms carrying energy, otherwise called heat. Atoms were regarded as imperceptibly small versions of ordinary solid particles following the usual laws of mechanics. For classical physicists and chemists, they were the entities that really underlay the phenomenal world and were discovered in the same way fields had been discovered: mathematically in imagination.

The mathematical models devoid of pictorial content that are typical of modern science resulted from attempts to fit the concepts of atoms and waves to the discoveries made at the end of the nineteenth century that led to quantum theory. Although atoms and waves lost, in this theory, their physical, commonsensical qualities, they still seemed useful in discovering new mathematics. Our mathematics has guided us into realms of the world in which the concepts of mechanics with which we started are no longer applicable. As long as the pictures of wave and particle are regarded only as analogies, just as the elastic forces were analogies for fields of force, they are useful. The danger lies in our becoming secretly and unconsciously convinced of the reality of these pictures despite paying lip service to their model nature. The models then prevent us from taking the next necessary step to recognition of the quantum and relativistic worlds for what they are: completely new and previously occult realms of experience in which, to begin with, we can find our way only with mathematics as a guide.

In this situation we can take courage from what Max Planck wrote in his scientific autobiography:

> My original decision to devote myself to science was a direct result of the discovery which has never ceased to fill me with enthusiasm since my early youth—the comprehension of the far-from-obvious fact that the laws of human reasoning coincide with the laws governing the sequence of impressions we receive from the world about us; that, therefore, pure reasoning can enable humanity to gain an insight into the mechanism of the latter.

And from Einstein's exclamation "I want to know how God created this world.... I want to know his thoughts."

Following these originators of modern scientific thought, we shall in the next chapters continue the scientific quest. However, we shall attempt to employ *all* our faculties in an interplay between the senses and thought. Our guide in developing new ideas, including mathematical ones, will be the historical development of mechanics out of body-sense experience.

4. Conscious Participation

Modern people regard themselves as having recently awakened from a dreamlike mythological consciousness that persisted through the Middle Ages. Myths are like dreams; while living in them we do not question their logic. Yet once we awake, such logic is usually rejected as unsuitable for gaining understanding of the outer world. Being awake means being confronted by experience, which we seek to understand through our thinking. This thinking has actually already begun when we see anything as a specific "thing." Our thinking activity provides the concepts and mental pictures to match the percepts coming from the world around us. Because this happens, to begin with, before we are even conscious of trying to understand the world, we must, as waking human beings, also be critical of our own mental activity: we must be prepared to question whether the mental pictures that accompany outer experiences are appropriate. And when we examine outer experience we must always select *one* aspect from a manifold of *many* possibilities. Only when we remain conscious of all these possibilities are we truly awake. A scientific relationship with the physical world can be thought of as a state of equilibrium in which the investigator must balance focused attention with an awareness of the whole within which the subject under investigation is found. Maintaining this equilibrium can prevent scientists from falling asleep and forgetting the processes and experiences that make knowledge possible in the first place. From this point of view, and bearing in mind the conclusion of chapter three, we recognize the danger that models may become myths on which the mind dwells. Ancient myths are divorced from sense experience. In a similar manner, modern scientific models are removed from the original perceptions that inspired the thoughts upon which these same models were formed.

In the following pages we give examples of how to "meet phenomena scientifically" while remaining in the state of "scientific equilibrium" just described. The examples we give lead to a new understanding of the wave-particle enigma of modern physics and show it to be merely an artifact of model-oriented science. (For a historical, philosophical, and linguistic discussion of conscious and unconscious participation see Barfield [1988].)

A Thunderstorm and Acoustics

As a first example we consider a thunderstorm. From the many different phenomena of such a storm, concepts for the science of acoustics can be developed. To begin with, we see the threatening blackness of the clouds and feel the peculiar atmosphere of tension. Ominous rumblings can be heard in the distance. Then come the first gusts of wind turning leaves over. The first heavy drops of rain splash on the ground, and a flash of lightning announces a deluge.

Rather than directing our thinking toward a description of the storm, we could, of course, focus on its onset as narrated in the weather report or as it is portrayed on a television weather map. Alternatively, we might follow the rapid drop of the barometer. We might remember the sultry heat earlier in the day, so different from the usual freshness of the morning air, and the brassy sun seeming too near for comfort. Or, we might direct our attention to the psychological effects of the storm, both on human beings and animals.

Given these many possibilities, we must choose which aspect of the thunderstorm we wish to attend to. In this instance we concern ourselves with the audible and visible phenomena of thunder and lightning. The storm we are considering began with a rumbling in the distance, which was followed by the first flash of lightning. Other storms are foreshadowed by silent sheet lightning stretching across and illuminating the distant horizon. Watching the spectacle as it nears us, we see the bright figures of lightning flashes and become aware of their increasing extent. At the same time, the thunder becomes louder. In its rumblings we begin to distinguish individual sound formations. After an initial clap the heavens seem to resound as if they were gigantic vaults. Thunder is perceived as a sound image, just as are melodies.

In the train of thought just pursued, description evolved into reflections on those concepts that seemed to fit the experience. Our interest in the qualities perceived naturally awakens thoughts. Realizing that sound images can be seen as figures extended in the dimension of time, we go on to compare them with the two-dimensional images imprinted in our field of vision, which are like outlines in light, lacking depth.

When storms are fully under way, the sequence of visible lightning and audible thunder becomes quite definite. There is a regularity in the way thunder follows lightning. This is not the case when lightning follows thunder. As the storm approaches, the interval between lightning and subsequent thunder becomes shorter; when the storm is overhead and lightning strikes nearby, hardly any time passes between them. We surmise that lightning and the immediately following thunder belong together. They are related, while thunder and any lightning that may follow immediately are not. We begin to see lightning and thunder as different aspects of a *single* phenomenon that has a spatial extension grasped through the phenomenon's existence in time. Sounds are heard later the farther away they are generated. This principle is a key to acoustics, where the concept of the speed of sound connects spatial and temporal aspects of sound.

Scientific Thinking Leads to General Concepts

These considerations may seem somewhat capricious. We do not usually combine dramatic experience of nature with thoughts about the fields of perception gained through our sense organization. It is more common to think about sense experiences later on, after the experience itself. This is the way scientists truly live with a subject. After first meeting an astonishing phenomenon they try to remember the scene and are all the more attentive when they get a chance to witness it or a similar phenomenon again. Giving thought to the circumstances, they then become aware of concepts that order the circumstances rationally. Here they may find aspects of the phenomenon to be identical or similar to other phenomena. They are then led to test with experiments their understanding of these conceptual relationships.

The sound of thunder reminds us of echoes we have heard elsewhere. Hence, the same concepts used to explain echoes serve us here. Just as we learned to judge our distance from a cliff by the time required for it to reflect our call, so we learn to judge the distance of the visible lightning discharges by the time elapsed before we hear the associated thunderclap.

But the mere concept of a speed of sound in air will not suffice to found a science of acoustics. There are further questions: What of the quality of sound, of its loudness or its pitch? The "sharpness" of a clap of thunder reveals a storm's proximity; a deep "growling" signifies great distance. A clap may be very loud, while growling thunder is noticed only when we and our surroundings are very quiet.

Thinking about such phenomena can lead into new realms. With an echo, the concept of the "speed of sound" is a purely abstract construction. It arises in analogy to the usual concept of speed as distance covered by a physical object in time. Even though sound is not a body, why not imagine sound traveling through air anyway? This is done despite the fact that we neither see nor hear sound moving. Nevertheless, the model of sound traveling through air is a powerful picture used to compare audible experiences with visible ones in time and space. Once we have decided to use this model, we begin to watch for phenomena in which movement is really taking place. Approaching and moving past a playing brass band, we hear the pitch of the music change, just as the pitch of a siren on a fire engine changes as it speeds by. Even the blowing of wind can mold sound images, as we can hear when the volume of the peal of bells changes with a gust; it truly seems as if sound is carried by the wind.

Our thinking leads us further, to other concepts essential to acoustics, among them, the diminished loudness of sound as it spreads through space, frequency as applied to pitch, and the diminished loudness of higher-pitched sound propagating in air considered as a consequence of the effect of viscosity. When we are told that sound travels in the form of longitudinal waves of compressed and expanded air, then we should realize that this model, too, is the result of scientists living with questions arising from sense experience.

The Thunderstorm Again

We began our description of a thunderstorm from the point of view of an observer experiencing the storm vividly yet without at first having ready-made explanations. We saw how scientific curiosity could lead to general concepts, which, in turn, make other phenomena meaningful to us. In studying nature we gradually become aware of journeying in a landscape of seemingly endless variety. Countless paths, whose destinations are beyond our sight, branch off and entice us into new realms. We may even forget the question that first caught our interest. It often happens that we are then satisfied with a grasp of the main principles; in this case of acoustics, interest in the particular thunderstorm recedes into the background. In fact, the question could be asked, Why start with a thunderstorm? Why not begin with an experiment in which the speed of sound, its frequency, and its volume are measured electronically? Isn't the thunderstorm itself actually lost in scientific work anyway? Is what we have been considering of any importance for understanding lightning? It seems we might have been better off going to a laboratory for high-voltage discharges, where we might have been led on an expedition into the realm of plasma physics.

Our approach did give us insight into the nature of perceptual experience. We found ourselves comparing two-dimensional visual images with sound images, which unfold in the linear dimension of time. We came to realize that our spatial grasp of the approaching thunderstorm was given to us by neither our visual nor our auditory experience. Actually, a comparison created by our *thinking* was necessary in order for us to grasp its depth dimension. The effort of thinking merged the appearances so that we could become aware of the storm as an entity. This is how we began to "get in touch" with the storm.

The experience of lightning is so enigmatic because we seem to be witnessing the entry of a phenomenon into the physical world. Something appears where before there was nothing; an event is born into space. We feel we are witnessing an event on the verge of physical existence. We are startled not only by its entering the world completely without prior notice but also by its brevity. Our "getting in touch with it" is obviously retrospective!

Lightning can be understood as an archetypal event. Visually we experience a "striking" image, while in the ensuing thunder we experience the necessary consequences in time and space. More lasting consequences occur when lightning strikes a tree. In creating pictures of the process, our thinking makes the thunderstorm meaningful as a phase in the life of the landscape.

It seems strange to modern human beings to find the experience of nature interwoven with the process of gaining scientific understanding. It appears that the objective and the subjective are being confused. Only the discovery of general laws and the exact description of events are generally accepted as scientific. However, when we abstract general law from the circumstances of actual individual experiences, we are ignoring parts of reality that are, nevertheless, valid aspects of any scientific endeavor. The scientist tends to replace the actual experience of events with imaginations of modeled events in order to preserve the fiction of a detached observer. These models are then often applied to experimental situations devised to accommodate the models. When the models seem to be validated by results from such an artificial environment, the question must be asked: Have we discovered something about nature or about our cleverness in designing environments to match models? In this chapter we are attempting to demonstrate that scientific results can also be achieved by an investigator who remains conscious of those aspects of human experience that inspired inquiry in the first place and of the faculties used to gain scientific understanding.

The Two Roots of Vision

As Aristotle pointed out, a minimal distance is necessary for distinct vision. An object that is so close to the eye that it is practically touching it is nearly invisible. If we try to view one of our fingers while it brushes against our eyelashes, we become aware of a dark, extremely blurred image. No distinct form can be seen because the lens cannot focus on a body practically touching it. And, incidentally, if daylight is to illuminate a scene, there must be space between object and eye. Since vision relies essentially on relationships in space, it invites understanding in geometrical terms. For an image to be distinct, its outlines must be distinguishable as boundaries between areas of different color or brightness. These qualities have nothing to do with distance or focusing. The blue sky cannot be brought into focus. Color and brightness are not of a geometrical nature. They are qualities perceptible to vision alone. One could even argue that the spatial context of vision is incidental, the essence of vision lying elsewhere. For the remainder of this chapter we will be occupied with the two roots of vision: the one spatial and the other pertaining to color and brightness. Gradually we will move from one to the other and see that the so-called wave-particle paradox is a consequence of not making this distinction.

Looking at a Lake

Standing at the edge of a lake, we can choose to direct our attention to two different views: the surroundings of the water or the water itself. The images we see around the lake are those of objects that can be touched as well as seen, while those in the water can only be seen. Usually, when we view an object we also know where it is located and what it will feel like. We go to it confidently and succeed in our first attempt to touch it. Our expectations concerning the hardness or softness, roughness or smoothness of the surface are seldom disappointed.

The situation is not so simple when we look at the water. The blue we see may be either the blue of the reflected sky or the blue of the clear water itself. It is usually easy to distinguish between the two by looking at the sky and the water's surface in turn. But we can also tell the difference by looking at the lake alone, because the image of the sky on the water is modified by every ripple on the surface. The blue of the water also shows a characteristic variation—dark at the center of the lake where the water is deepest and growing increasingly lighter until the pebbles at the bottom are visible close to shore. We shall first investigate the reflections and then turn to the phenomena we see when looking into the water.

Looking into Water—Reflections as Space Creators

An undisturbed water surface is necessary for clear reflections. In fact, it is the disturbances of reflections that draw our attention to the ripples. We do not usually see ripples directly—that is, as moving crests and troughs; we see constantly disturbed reflections. This becomes clear when the sky is gray and featureless. Here we see ripples only near the shore as they disturb the outlines of reflected images of trees and bushes; ripples are not visible where only the bright, undifferentiated sky is reflected or the dark mass of vegetation.

Let us now look at reflected images in more detail. It is easiest to start with our own image. Stepping right to the edge of the water, bending forward and looking down into the water, we can distinguish a familiar face (at least in its reflected image) directly beneath us looking up. It is small compared with our feet, one of which can be made to block out the image of the face—even though, in actuality, a foot is narrower than a face.

When we look at someone standing across from us at the edge of the lake, the image in the water is always connected with the flesh-and-blood figure above it. As we walk along the shore, the figure of flesh and blood and its reflection stay united. When viewed up close, the reflection seems smaller and dimmer than the figure of flesh and blood. However, when we bend down and our eyes draw near the level of the water, the two figures approach equality in size and brightness. Viewed at water level, there appears to be almost exact symmetry. The apparent changes in size are the same as those caused by changes in perspective. What is farther away seems to be smaller. Was the head of our own image smaller than our feet because it was farther away? As long as we are standing upright, looking at someone else, the reflection is farther from our eyes than the figure of flesh and blood. Are reflection and flesh-and-blood figure equidistant when we bend down to the water's surface?

These questions tempt us to measure the depth of the reflected images from the water's surface. If we try to use a measuring stick, a number of difficulties arise. When we dip the stick into the water, we probably find that the water near the shore is not deep enough for the stick to reach the head of the image. This gives us the idea that we should try the measurement farther out in a boat or, perhaps, in the laboratory, where conditions more amenable to measurement can be arranged. However, another look at the measuring stick as we push it into the water makes us hesitate. We note that the divisions in the water seem smaller than those not yet immersed; it is as if the calibration lines were lifted toward the water's surface and compressed. The end of the stick in the water is apparently not moving as fast as we are pushing it down! Inadvertently we are already looking at an object inside the water rather than at reflections. However, we see not only that part of the stick that is in the water, we see also the reflection of the upper part of the stick not yet immersed. The markings in the reflection are, within perspective, the same as those of the measuring stick. Accordingly, the reflected image might be measured with the reflection of the measuring stick and not with the immersed stick. We therefore ask the person at the edge of the lake to hold a long measuring stick vertically with the zero mark at water level. When we then look at the figure with the measuring rod, we find that the reflected image of the object appears to reach as far below the water's surface as the object is above it.

If we really want to be scientific about our activity, we should stop at this point and question our reasoning. Of course, we could have anticipated this result, for we had already decided upon it the moment we took the reflected measuring stick to be the measure. When did we really begin to grasp the concept of symmetry between reflected space and ordinary space? This was certainly during that phase of our studies when we observed how perspective changes when we view reflected images. We recognized then that the same laws that are familiar to us in ordinary space apply also to reflected space.

We are now ready to describe the phenomenon of reflection geometrically. Reflection in the water creates a visual space below the surface in which objects are visible but are not tangible. For every object above the surface there is one below, apparently as far from the surface as the one above. The laws of perspective in this reflected space are the same as those in the space containing tangible bodies.

An elegant demonstration of this can be set up in the laboratory using a glass surface as a mirror instead of water. A thin glass plate is supported horizontally with a cup set on it. An identical cup is held under the plate with its base in contact with the glass. In suitable lighting it is possible to move the bottom cup, which is visible through the glass, so that one sees it fit exactly into the reflected image of the top cup. This coincidence of cup and image perseveres under all viewing angles.

From these experiences we can now formulate the laws of reflection more generally. If we imagine an observer confronted with a plane mirror surface, we can say that there exists a space on the "back side" of the reflecting surface that we shall call the *reflected image space.* The space on the "observer's side" we shall call the *tangible body space.* For every point in the tangible body space, there exists a corresponding point in the reflected image space. Corresponding points are equidistant from the mirror plane. The laws of perspective are the same for the two spaces.

The tangible body and reflected image spaces are only visually symmetric. Objects in the tangible body space are touchable as well as visible, while objects in the reflected image space are only visible. The symmetry of the situation can also be described in this way: the observer sees the reflected image exactly as the reflected image of the observer would see the tangible body image. Views from one space to the other are identical.

Earlier in this chapter we suggested that a scientific relationship with the physical world can be understood as a state of equilibrium in which the investigator balances a focus of attention on one aspect with an awareness of the whole from which it is drawn. It is just this sort of equilibrium that we have been practicing. By using our "body senses" in association with our own movements to watch for changes in the images of the directly seen world and the reflected one, we have gained a mathematical law (that of mirror sym-metry) of the physics of reflection. It may be difficult for the reader to recognize that what we have been doing is truly scientific, but that is because contemporary human beings are mesmerized by the expectation that scientific description be impersonal. The physics of reflection is ordinarily taught in terms of light rays that elastically bounce off plane surfaces. But light rays are here merely hypothetical entities used solely to support the bias of impersonal scientific description.

Before setting up any laboratory demonstration of the law of mirror symmetry as it applies to reflection, it was first necessary to grasp the appropriateness of the concept of mirror space through the experience of reflection phenomena in nature. Without this recognition we would never have thought of the demonstration with the glass surface and identical cups. Once experienced, however, the demonstration is eloquent and compelling without having to resort to hypothetical entities with hypothetical properties (such as the elastic bouncing of "light rays" from plane surfaces).

Perhaps we should also mention another aspect of mirror images that makes them feel strange: Why is it so difficult to do things while watching one's activity only in the mirror? Somehow the view impedes us in our movements, giving us bad advice in a mischievous way. (Try to tie the knot in your shoelace while you look at your own hands at work in a mirror.) Even if we know the law of mirror-image space intellectually, we are not yet accustomed to its implications with respect to real life. Mirror symmetrical forms are by no means identical!

Looking into Water—Visible and Tangible Objects No Longer Coincide

Looking at the measuring stick in the previous section, we realized that the shape and size of objects appear different when we see them under water. In addition, various color effects can be noticed. We consider the geometrical aspects first.

Imagine a water-filled trough, such as a fish tank, with a horizontal base. If we want to retrieve a coin lying on the bottom of the tank, we must roll up our sleeves farther than expected if we are to keep them dry. Just as with the calibrations on the measuring stick, the coin appears to be "lifted," or closer to the surface than it is to the touch. Visible and tangible objects no longer coincide. When we walk around the tank, the bottom appears to move; wherever we stand it seems to slope downward toward us. Thus, for each tangible object there are apparently a number of visual ones. The position of objects appears to change with the position of the observer. But as long as the observer's eyes are kept level at the same height above the surface, a measuring stick placed vertically within the water will remain vertical and the image of any object will be suspended directly above where the object can be touched.

Other experiments show that the image-lifting effect depends on the respective media in which object and observer are situated. If, for instance, the object is embedded in a block of glass, it will seem nearer to the observer than an object in an equal depth of water. In both cases, of course, the observer is situated in the air outside.

The image, or visual space under water for tangible objects in water, can be described geometrically for any observer. Assume your eyes are perpendicular to the water's surface. We now have to consider two different spaces below the surface of the water: touch space and sight space. For every object in sight space there is a corresponding object below it in touch space. The distance from the visible object to the water's surface above it will be less than the distance from the tangible object to the water's surface. Furthermore, the ratio of these two distances will be the same for all pairs of corresponding visual and tangible objects. (Those readers familiar with physics will recognize the inverse of this ratio as the refractive index of the media in which observer and object are situated.) If we continue along these lines we will discover that this is true for all angles of observation.

We have now arrived at a version of the basic law of refraction attributed to Willebrord Snell (1580–1626). This version is based on the phenomenon of images of immersed objects "floating up" or being "lifted." Obviously, this situation is stranger than the one we encountered in viewing a reflection. Nevertheless, in order to study it we use similar methods. Standing up and then crouching down, we become aware of movements in the image we are investigating that our ordinary perspective would not have led us to expect. Such an experience is an encounter with water through our body senses.

We can again be on the lookout for other situations in which we might have a chance to make this encounter more conscious. Standing on the banks of a mountain stream, we may notice the water rising and falling regularly, while the stones at the edge appear, alternately, to be submerged more deeply and then almost to touch the surface. As water flows toward the shore, the image of the stones seems to rise and then sink down again as the water recedes. If we really concentrate we can gain the impression that the water is raising the ground it periodically engulfs. Such observations can keep us aware of how the introduction of a denser optical medium modifies our visual experience. Indeed, the perceived changes are exactly the same as would result from the application of a physical force with our hands—that is, from moving the stones closer.

Looking back to our study of reflections, we can clearly see the steps involved. We paid little heed to the water itself. In peering through the surface, however, looking inside, we became involved with the water. We went from reflection to refraction and the experience became stronger. Nevertheless, we were able to restrict our attention to the location and shape of visible images. Of course, the images are visible by virtue of being light and dark and by the coloring they assume.

Looking into Water—Color Aspects

Now let us change our focus and consider colors seen in the lake. We already noticed that the blue of the water changes with its depth. Although they are not nearly as obvious, we may notice other colors when we look at the bottom of the lake and at the rocks and pebbles. Close observation reveals that the edges of objects at the bottom are sometimes blurred and fringed with narrow bands of color. The fringes become more pronounced as the edges appear more raised. Although the colors may be brilliant, especially in bright sunlight, they are easily overlooked because the fringes are so narrow. Once they are noticed, they appear like narrow openings into a new, magical world of color.

Imagine we are looking at a submerged white tile leaning against the side of a large tank of water. We view the tile from the opposite side against a dark background. As we bend down to bring our eyes near the surface, the image of the tile will rise while shrinking in its vertical extension. Its upper edge will blur, turning into a blue

fringe from which a violet haze radiates up into the dark
above it. The lower edge will turn into a red fringe, over
which a yellow haze darkens the adjacent white of the tile
above it. The two basic fringes and hazes develop simultaneously as the image rises. A dark object on a white background would develop the same colors, but with the
locations reversed.

If the tile is short enough in height, the haze from below
will eventually impinge on the fringe above it. Their colors
will react: yellow and blue producing green, magenta forming through the reaction of violet with red. The six colors
produced are always the same: violet, cyan (or light blue),
green, yellow, red, and magenta. These six colors can be
arranged in a circle (rather than in a band). While the
color with which we start this circular arrangement is arbitrary, the sequence of colors is not; it is a product of direct
color experience. Intermediate shades can easily be pictured leading from one color to another. For example,
between violet and cyan we can picture indigo, ultramarine,
and many shades of blue, but not green; between yellow
and red there are all the oranges, but not violet. Moreover,
wherever we start, the end color of the series is a neighbor
of the first. Between the magenta and violet in the series
cited, there are various shades of pink that are more red or
more blue respectively, the nearer they are to the magenta
or to the violet. These observations are consistent with
arranging the colors in a circle rather than in a series.

On our excursion into the realm of color via looking
into a lake, we departed from the spatial aspect of experience. Colors are discerned only with the sense of sight. It is
also through this sense that brightness and darkness are
apprehended. In looking into the water or through a glass
prism, colors appear at the expense of distinct contours in

vision. But it is just these contours that give our body senses access to the seen world, thus making it measurable in terms of angles and space. Apparently, when viewing color through a transparent medium we are somehow "removed from space." How does this happen? The same process that lifts visible images also apparently modifies the boundaries of adjacent contrasting areas in vision. Colors appear to be created by the raising effect water has on the images of submerged touchable objects. In other words, the whole process seems to remove the perception of color from the experience of clearly outlined physical bodies. However, as science is usually practiced, the criterion for reality is based on just this experience of bodies. Nevertheless, people who actually work with color find themselves in a realm where relationships are determined by the laws of color (the color circle, for example) rather than any abstract spatial models.

It is significant that "lawful relations" in the realm of color are best discovered through the processes that give rise to the colors in the first place, and not through manipulations that treat the colors as already existing objects for our perception. Unlike laws of physical bodies, color relationships are inseparable from the conditions under which colors arise; they are, so to speak, laws of becoming. In a very general sense, we could compare color processes to those of chemistry. At least this is true if we cease imagining chemical processes as rearrangements in the way very little marbles are stuck together—that is, if we remain with our actual perceptions and refrain from imagining a model of atoms thought to be more real. We may then notice that changes in color can be just as important in the experience and practice of chemistry as the "bodily" aspects, such as weight, which are portrayed by the atomic picture.

Although we left tactile reality, we nevertheless stayed within the bounds of logically formulated mathematical relations. In the color circle, such relations are represented by geometrical forms used symbolically. In the sense we realized at the end of the previous chapter, they represent a model with no underlying perceptual content. They are purely mathematical, but nevertheless qualitative means of discovering relationships.

In Search of Real Color

Imagine you are gazing vacantly at a sheet of paper on which your red pencil is lying. If you lift the pencil after ten or fifteen seconds, a shimmering bar of bluish green will remain as an afterimage. If a box of crayons is at hand, you could produce afterimages in sequence: light blue bringing forth orange; violet, greenish yellow; magenta, green; and vice versa. (Bright lighting is not required for these appearances.)

There is another phenomenon in which colors appear that are oppositely situated in a color circle. It is easily observed toward sunset in a snow-covered landscape. The snow has the colors of the setting sun, yellow to pink. The colors of the tree shadows vary from violet to green. At each instant the colors of the snow and the adjacent shadows are opposite in the same color circle. Pairs of colors, as they are produced in afterimages and in the colored shadows just described, are called physiological complementaries. The process of producing afterimages is called successive contrast, while colored shadows are produced by simultaneous contrast.

These contrast phenomena are always with us. For instance, grayish surfaces are always tinged with the color that is complementary to the dominant background color. In the case of a seascape this dominant background is blue. A dominant background makes it possible for a small, unobtrusively colored area—a pillow on a sofa for example—to change its appearance according to the color of its surroundings. Because color is so strongly affected by illumination, it is wise to view fabrics and clothing by daylight before deciding on a purchase. Colored illumination can produce very surprising results. Two pieces of fabric may look alike in incandescent light but dissimilar in fluorescent light. Moreover, fabric may appear very different under illumination from various light sources that seem to generate very similar colors.

What happens when we look at the colored fringes mentioned in the last section with colored illumination? They are also modified by the color of the illumination. With yellow illumination, the violet will tend to disappear, becoming increasingly difficult to distinguish from a dark background, while the yellow haze also disappears, becoming increasingly difficult to distinguish from the white of the tile.

It is clear that there is no definite answer to the question, What is the color of this surface really? In fact, the question makes no sense. *Color is not something that exists independently of its surroundings.* The chemical nature of the surface, that is, the pigments it contains, is a very important determining factor. The physical properties of the surface, such as rough or smooth texture, also influence its appearance. Another factor is the illumination. What is usually forgotten is the human sense organ itself. Our sense of color seems to depend on the totality of the scene perceived. As we have observed, the color of a "beige" cushion varies with illumination as well as with the surroundings. The great German poet Goethe probably first noted that the total color experience tends to be harmonious, meaning that pronounced hues are balanced by their complementary color. Here, if one could imagine all the colors of a natural scene mixed, the result would be a neutral gray shade. This is taken into account when developing color photographic prints. The light to which the print paper is exposed is passed through three colored filters of variable density. In this way, color can be added to those produced by the negative. This is done in order that the "average color" of the print be neutral gray. However, if the technicians get it wrong, the eye will do its best to put the mistake right.

As we saw in chapter two, the direct experience of warmth depends on a "constant give-and-take between the body and its surroundings." The experience conveyed is based on the interaction between the sense organ and what it perceives. The sense of color acts in a very similar way. What it "perceives" in one part of the field of view depends on its interaction (frequently an unobserved interaction) with other parts. There is, however, an important difference between the action of the two senses. The perception of warmth requires an exchange between the sense and the surroundings. The perception of color depends on changes in the scene, the field of vision itself.

Geometrical Representations of Nonspatial Qualities

We have lingered in the realm of color in order to show a few of the manifold ways in which color percepts are related to a whole. The appearance of colored fringes, afterimages, and colored shadows leads us to associate pairs of colors, The simplest representation of the "whole" that includes the phenomena in which complementary colors arise is the *color circle.*

Obviously, the human eye is very much involved in all the phenomena described. In one way or another, it is an essential element in every situation where color effects are considered. Of course, a light source is also required. Nevertheless, it *is* possible to study aspects of color phenomena without an explicit study of the physiology of the eye or of the physics of emission and absorption. Of course, certain effects may point to the role of the eye. If, for example, different individuals cannot agree on what is perceived, then it would be necessary to consider the various forms of color blindness. At some point it might also be appropriate to compare the effects of natural and artificial illuminations. Using a sodium vapor lamp we would no longer see colors otherwise visible in daylight. Such perception might then stimulate our interest in the spectra of gases and spectroscopy. In such a study it is the visible spectrum, that is, the pattern dark, red, green, violet, dark, that is taken to be the most fitting representation, for it orders emitted radiation between red and violet on a linear scale that can readily be used as a gauge for energy levels.

In the representations described, a geometrical form (circle or line) symbolizes the totality that takes into account all possible manifestations of the quality under investigation (colors of a natural scene or colors arising from spectral emissions).

Relationships in the realm of color can be clearly understood with concepts permitting mathematical representation. (The system of color measurement established by the *Commission Internationale de l'Eclairage*, or CIE, is the accepted standard.) No one expects such mathematical descriptions of color relationships, however, to be explanations in the form of descriptions of underlying mechanisms, as, for example, when atoms are used as explanations of macroscopic effects. In fact, in the case of mechanics no one expects such explanations either. Could it not be that *explanations in terms of underlying mechanisms are not really required anywhere in physics?* (In atomic and subatomic physics, principles are found that can be formulated mathematically. These are concepts, such as the Pauli exclusion principle and the Heisenberg uncertainty relations, needing no underlying mechanisms to explain them. New realms are found. They are not a substitute, however, for the experience of the previously known realm.)

Independent Physical Principles Cooperate

As we saw in chapter three, Galileo went a step beyond Aristotle in thinking of acceleration and motion independent of the process of friction. Although they work together in our everyday experience of mechanics, as described by Aristotle, they need not do so under all conditions. Thus, all objects that fall in a vacuum accelerate identically. In contrast, objects falling in a viscous medium tend to travel at a constant speed determined by their shape, weight, and the fluid character of the medium.

Obviously, both phenomena take place under conditions in which "weight" can be observed; both are forms of vertical downward movement in the direction of gravity. Since we are well accustomed to situations of varying friction, it is easy for us to follow Galileo's thought when he distinguishes between these principles. He grasped that they are governed by independent laws, each expressing idealized relationships of different conceptual content.

In the field of optics, scientists were less eager to separate principles. We are accustomed to relating our bodily senses to bodies. It is easy to become irritated by light's lack of bodily attributes when studying optics. That "lack" has made it even more difficult to intuit a distinction just as important as that between acceleration caused by gravity and the effects friction has on motion. We have in mind the distinction between wave optics and quantum mechanics, the two independent aspects of light cooperating in every optical phenomenon. When this is understood, the wave-particle duality is no longer paradoxical. This is the question with which we end this chapter.

We often use a camera instead of the eye, replacing the retina with a photographic emulsion and the eye's lens with the camera's. Manufactured in a chemical plant, the photographic emulsion must be returned to a chemical laboratory for processing. The lens is a product of industry, where special shapes are ground and polished to standards of utmost precision. Similarly, the camera itself is a product of fine mechanical workmanship and electronic materials manufacturing.

Here we have two realms, the fields of photochemistry and mathematical optics. Although both are necessary to photography, they remain distinct; there is no melting together. For a scientist to become proficient in either, long years of study in different university departments, along with practical experience in totally unlike fields, are required.

When these fields cooperate, photographic images such as color slides, prints, and posters can be produced that represent a view the eye might have seen directly. In the eye itself the retina cooperates with the rest of the organ. In a similar way, in physics we speak of "generalized coordinates," which are independent variables that describe the condition of a system. For example, the pressure and temperature of a body can be varied independently of each other, although the state of the body depends on them both. Such "cooperation of independent realms" is *the* essential trait of the *physical* world—that is, the inorganic world. In the following sections, we shall consider the two independent, but cooperating fields of photochemistry and mathematical optics in order to see what relationships are intended when speaking of waves of light, on the one hand, and of quanta of light, on the other. To what realms do these concepts belong?

A Visit to the Realm of Imaging

A camera is suitably focused if its lens projects a distinct image onto the plane of the film. If we could become ants and wander around on the image plane, moving from one area of color to another, we would not have a view of the whole of the image. All we could observe would be the lens, which would look like a round window of opaque material. Its apparent size would be determined by the diaphragm's setting and distance from the image plane. Wherever an ant might be located, the lens would appear to be of uniform color and brightness. If the ant then crawled across the image plane into a different region of color and "looked up," it would find that the lens now appeared to be a different color. Between the two regions the ant would gradually cross a border that would always appear slightly blurred. Taking into account that adjacent areas in the image correspond to adjacent fields in the scene, we understand that the lens is connecting areas on the image plane with fields in the scene. If, for example, colored bulbs of an electric sign are in the scene, then an area on the film in the image plane will be "directly connected" with those bulbs. The lens bridges the gulf between film and scene by bringing some part of the film into a one-to-one relationship with some part of the scene. We can say that the distance between scene and film has, in a sense, been virtually cancelled.

What principles govern the phenomena of imaging? They can best be learned by considering the precision of an image and how it is enhanced. Even with a camera optimally focused and having a lens of ideal quality, edges of adjacent areas on the image will be somewhat blurred. We might suspect this could be remedied by focusing the camera more exactly. But even at optimum focusing there is still some blur. We usually expect clearer pictures to result from a smaller diaphragm opening because of the increased depth of field. So we are surprised to see the blur growing broader as the diaphragm is closed. Actually, the most distinct image is formed when the diaphragm is wide open! In this case a uniform area in the image corresponds to one in the scene with the greatest precision.

To understand this, physicists had to realize that an area *A* in the image is uniformly illuminated by the *entire area* of the lens even though area *A* corresponds only to the area *B* in the scene. This principle can be understood with the help of the accompanying diagram. All paths from *A* to *B* via the lens are understood to have something in common. This "something" is called the "optical distance" from *A* to *B*.

A simple imaging lens is of convex form. Although the connection along a straight path from *A* to *B* through the middle of the lens is the most direct, it must pass through the thickest layer of glass. In contrast, the path from *A* to *B* passing through the edge of the lens seems to be a detour but passes through the least thickness of glass. The concept of optical distance considers distances through the glass of the lens to be longer than those through air. In fact, "optical distances" are weighted according to the refractive index (a measure of the amount of "lifting" of images encountered when we looked into water) of the transparent material used to make a lens. Now the direct path traverses the thick center of the lens, while the path through the edge passes only through a thin section of glass. Thus the two light paths can have equal "optical distance" even though the spatial distances differ.

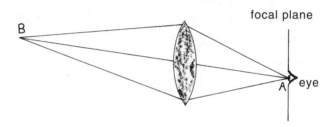

The basic principle is that *optical connections through spatial separation rely on paths of uniform optical distance.* As the ant moves from one place to the next, it will gradually sever its ties to the previous source of illumination and establish contact with a new one. Outside its previous position in the focal plane there is no connection to the previous source. In other words, at the ant's new location, paths of unlike optical distance connected with the original source would be blocked. The criterion of equal optical distance will become more and more stringent the wider the lens is opened, because there will be more paths through the lens whose lengths must be equal. (Compare the center path to the other paths in the diagram.) The best criterion would tell us precisely how much inhomogeneity in optical length can be tolerated before paths become obstructed and a blur results at the edge of an illuminated region. This criterion is given as a fraction of what is called the wavelength of light. Every color has a characteristic value.

Wavelength, a number, gives us a gauge for dimension in optical instruments. In the model for light, waves are pictured as traveling from B to A, being focused by the lens. In the development of modern physics it became clear that the amplitude of a "wave" was not a quantity that could be "perceived" directly. In fact, the "wave" itself is not a physical entity. All the same, it is a very powerful mathematical tool! On our visit to the realm of imaging we have encountered a field where mathematical reasoning provides a sound basis for understanding.

A Visit to the Realm of Chemical Action at a Distance

At dawn the Sun's brightness illuminates the landscape, and the colors of nature appear. Light can be thought of as the agent through which the Sun and the landscape cooperate. What is more, our own eyes take part in this union, giving us access to the visible world.

Although the Sun's illumination may seem to change without leaving its mark on nature, actually it does mold nature's appearance through the course of the year. Vegetation sprouts and grows in spring and summer. Fields are harvested. We ourselves may experience a severe sunburn after exposure in higher altitudes or at the seashore. Or, more subtly, we may experience the development of afterimages in our eyes. In the photographic process images are fixed. They are turned into patterns made of physical dyes. In all of these processes the meeting between illuminant and an illuminated object leads to temporary or enduring modifications. This is the field of photochemistry.

Photochemical effects may reveal an illuminant in several ways. There is, for example, a relationship between the cause of an afterimage and its visible effect, the afterimage itself. Photographic processing has been refined to perfection in order to render color prints nearly identical in color to the scene viewed by the camera. Adequate exposure of film can be achieved with different settings of the diaphragm if the different intensities are then compensated for with shorter or longer exposures. Within certain limits this is true. With respect to *quantity*, the film's degree of exposure to a given scene results from the size of the cone of light with which the lens illuminates the film multiplied by the length of time the shutter is open. This relationship is similar, though not identical, to the way water runs from a tap. The more one opens the tap, the greater the flow of water per second and the less time it takes to fill a bucket. Therefore, we are close to using the mental picture of a stream of water for a model of the intensity of illumination. It is insufficient, however, to characterize illumination only by its intensity; its *quality*—that is, its potential to direct a photochemical process in the direction of a specific color—must also be specified in some way. A model for this might be a "colored stream of water."

This model was unacceptable to physicists. With no perceptual qualities in the space between an illuminant and an illuminated object, they must have felt that a stream of visible quality was an unrealistic model. So they transformed the stream into an "invisible state" still imagined as being able to carry color, that is, a quality otherwise perceptible only to our sense of sight. This "invisible state" was then said to be a quantity of energy, or, more precisely, a distribution of quantities of energy. Thus a quantity of quantities was to be imagined flowing through space. The

↓

mental picture used to explain the relationship between illuminant and illumined object became this: quanta of energy are exchanged in a density appropriate to the actual intensity of light or color. This mental picture seemed to receive support when it was observed that electricity was emitted from an illuminated photocell. (We here refer to the photoelectric effect, whose role in the development of quantum mechanics was discussed in chapter three.) Violet illumination led to a higher electrical potential than did blue; blue illumination led to a higher electrical potential than did yellow. Hence, the color quality of light could be transformed into an electrical potential. Since electrical potential is measurable, it is possible to relate a measurement to illumination. However, this measurement is associated only with a mental model (quanta of optical energy moving from illuminant to illuminated body), which pictures a relationship accessible to thought alone. There is no way for us to observe the progress of an optical quantum from one body to another. The sole purpose of the concept of optical quanta is to "permit" effects on an illuminated body to be caused by an illuminant. The illuminant and the illuminated body must be specific materials with particular characteristics. They cannot be imagined, they must physically exist. In contrast to the overwhelmingly mathematical nature of imaging, chemical action at a distance is intimately related to materials.

In the 1920s, physicists realized that two different models for optical phenomena, arising from work in two different contexts, had been found. It was not possible to imagine these models simply as different aspects of the same physical-spatial entity. Furthermore, the physicists came to the conclusion that both principles worked in their respective realms: waves in optical imaging and quanta in the absorption and emission of energy from matter. They discovered that either a "wave nature" or a "quantum nature" could be revealed in any given experiment and that it was not possible to reveal both at the same time.

The surroundings of a radiating body, not the body itself, govern its relationship to other bodies. These boundary conditions "channel," so to speak, the illuminating effect along paths. The mathematics that express the laws of illumination can be derived from the model of "waves of light" (although other ways of deriving them are also possible).

On the other hand, the appropriate concept for emission and absorption processes is that of the quantization of energy. Quantization relates solely to bodies of specific chemical and specific thermal states. Unlike the laws of illumination, these quantum laws are not concerned with the spatial surroundings of the bodies. The appropriate model for this situation is that of energy states and their transitions.

The two realms we are here concerned with (illumination, and absorption and emission connected by illumination) are conceptually and phenomenally independent. The two realms became entangled, however, when physicists searched for a picture derived from the physical body experience of mechanics. They defined an elementary particle, called a photon, which was then taken to represent the quantum of energy exchangeable between bodies. As a particle, however, it implies bodylike qualities going far beyond those of an exchange of energy. A single pellet of lead shot is not only exchanged between the gun and the target; it is also transported through space. In the same way, the photon is imagined to be transported from one body to another. This formulation is, however, completely hypothetical and totally unnecessary. Worse, it is misleading, because it leads to paradoxes that seem to imply physics cannot be thought.

Earlier we described Einstein's "thought experiment" (see page 63) in which the appearance of *particle-like* results or *wavelike* results depends on the nature of the recording apparatus (mirrors or photographic emulsions) and not on the source of illumination. In other words, when it is designed to record wavelike phenomena, our apparatus shows interference patterns. And when it is designed to discover particle-like phenomena, our apparatus records individual spots. Apparently, in situations such as these we see what we set out to see. But, then, we may ask, What is light itself? This question is paradoxical because it is formulated within a context that presupposes light to be a thing that moves through space. Such a thing cannot be reasonably imagined as being both continuous and discrete. Since the phenomena themselves, interference patterns and spots on photographic emulsions, cannot be faulted, it appears that it is the way we think about the phenomena that is faulty.

The reader will have realized by now that the problem lies in imagining light as if it were a thing possessing attributes like those of actual objects. But since light cannot, in fact, be seen, the conception of a light particle (photon) is merely a pseudo-phenomenon. The paradox of the wave-particle duality results from a conceptual failure in which the two now familiar independent realms of imaging and chemical action at a distance have been inappropriately bound together through the artifice of imagining light to be object-like and thus concrete and familiar. Instead, we can realize that when the mirrors are in place our concern is with imaging. The resulting pattern is then fully understood in terms of the geometry of the mirrors and mathematics of waves. Nothing else is required!

When, on the other hand, photographic emulsions replace the mirrors, the scientific question becomes one of chemical action at the illuminated emulsion through a distance. Here understanding is achieved by means of the concept of the amount of energy required to transform the film. As is usual when we are involved with material, in this case the emulsion, understanding is gained in terms of quantities of energy, whether quantized or not.

The failure of thinking suggested by quantum mechanical paradoxes lies in the misplaced attempt to understand phenomena in terms of pseudo-phenomenal things imagined to actually bring about effects. Instead, the method of conscious participation described in this chapter seeks to find conceptual relationships between conditions and phenomena. An abstract pseudo-phenomenal realm is not inserted as a barrier between human thinking and human experience of the actual phenomenal world.

Nineteenth-century science tried to unite the whole body of natural science under a single aspect: mechanics. Twentieth-century physics has shown that this plan is, in principle, infeasible. Even inside the limited field of optics we must follow up at least two different approaches that lead us into two distinct realms; each one is valid. The twentieth century is teaching us more than that: nature and humanity are becoming more and more involved in crises that are the result of our applying a "scientific" self-assurance appropriate only to one field: classical mechanics. We must learn to give up building all science on the basis of its success in the single realm of mechanics.

5. Science Coming of Age

In the first chapter of this book we raised several questions
regarding the apparent inability of science to incorporate
within itself a view of being human that is true to experience. In an age in which science and technology so per-
vade Western culture, there is an almost irresistible urge to
identify what is real only with those elements out of which
the world of physics has been built. But human beings
have been banished, so to speak, from this world. Consequently they increasingly experience themselves as onlook-
ers rather than as participants in it. In fact, as we have
pointed out, as scientists we cultivate the habit of mind of
the passive observer. No wonder human beings living in a
technical age are afflicted with existential dilemmas of
alienation and anxiety regarding the world, even as they
gain increasing power and control over it.

All this is a direct consequence of the well-known fact
that science limits itself to those aspects of the world that
are measurable. The reason for this limitation is usually

given as science's need to be objective. And, in fact, it is true—and powerfully so—that increasingly accurate measurement has served as a corrective in the development of scientific ideas. As erroneous theories are discovered, they can be either corrected or rejected. In addition, more accurate measurement has been a prod toward uncovering deeper layers of reality. Although there have been many false steps, the test of measurement has assured that the general trend of science has been—within the limits of reductionism—toward increasing knowledge. Because of this success, we tend to equate what is real with what is objective and what is objective with what is measurable.

Ignored in all this is the role of the human being in gaining objective knowledge. This view of knowledge implies that the knowing human subject should not and does not intrude in the objective world "being known." The human senses are taken as receptors of stimuli and human thinking as the independent creator of concepts.

Ironically, science both appeals to the data of the senses and simultaneously rejects them as being unreliable. In the first place, sense data are measured. Only sense experience amenable to measurement is therefore incorporated into science. That which is not measurable, that which is in essence qualitative, is taken to be mere subjective sensation. Measurable qualities are endowed with an objective reality presumed to be independent of the senses. However, we have shown that knowledge of measurables is as inextricably bound to the senses as is seeing color. In fact, the measurable qualities are based on what are, in a way, the most personally directed of the senses. They are the ones that tell us about our own bodies. Based on what we know of the world through our senses, we can see that *choosing to limit science only to those experiences that are measurable is a wholly arbitrary choice within the framework of the nature of sense experience.*

We are not, of course, claiming that there were not good reasons for limiting science to only the measurable aspects of reality. We have discussed in detail how limiting science to the measurable gave it a certainty already inherent in the experience of mathematics, and we could not deny that the subsequent history of physics bears out the wisdom of this choice. However, we now find ourselves in a situation where the same science that provided the basis for individual freedom by liberating human beings from the need for external authority has also banished human beings from the reality of its knowledge. But without self-knowledge, the possibility of freedom is made increasingly meaningless.

Given the extremity of this situation, it is essential to reexamine the scientific endeavor, bearing in mind that all human knowing, without exception, is founded on human faculties. Therefore, any limits we place on knowing—scientific or otherwise—presuppose a knowledge of these faculties. From this point of view the requirement that science be concerned only with measurable sense experience invites reexamination.

Mathematical Physics:
Exercise for the Development of Sense-free Thinking

The success of mathematical physics has been dramatic, profound, and undeniable. Beginning with Galileo in the seventeenth century and culminating three generations later in the work of Newton, mathematical physics was developed in order to describe the motion of bodies. As described in earlier chapters, mathematically analyzed elements were at first objects of actual experience; although idealized, they were directly observable parts of the phenomenal world. In the eighteenth century, for the first time, machines could be designed and manipulated in thought before they were actually built out of materials. This was made possible by the formulation of idealized general physical laws and was responsible for the subsequent rapid rise in technology.

Technology's early success led to the conviction that all processes in nature were mechanical. Mechanisms were assumed to be at work everywhere in nature, "behind" all phenomena. The physicist imagined microscopic mechanisms as being responsible for the appearance of what was actually observed in the phenomenal macroscopic world. Such thought models, being mechanical, could be analyzed mathematically. Even the phenomena of electricity at first yielded to this procedure. We described how Faraday imagined a field of force based on the analogy of an elastic space. Maxwell then mathematized Faraday's notion of a field using the analogy of a flowing fluid. The value of imagined mechanisms as vehicles for the relationships between phenomena was clearly demonstrated.

Early in the twentieth century, physicists introduced a profound change in this procedure. In order to describe and explain certain phenomena, they found it necessary to imagine models with elements that behaved in ways that had no counterpart at all in the world of phenomena. That is, the mechanism was not only invisible but also consisted of elements that behaved like nothing in the world as it is actually experienced. For example, electrons were imagined as jumping from one orbit to another instantaneously under the action of a quantum of energy while crossing a region in which the probability of their existence is zero.

This is not how an ordinary charged particle behaves. Also, an ordinary orbiting charged particle emits electromagnetic waves continuously, thereby gradually losing energy and spiraling down to its center of attraction rather than remaining in a fixed orbit. In addition, a quantum, or finite amount of energy that can be transferred instantaneously, does not exist in the world of sense-perceptible particles and waves. The quantum of energy was arbitrarily "thought up" to make the mathematics "work out" according to experiment. Thus, the thought pictures no longer conformed to sense-perceptible reality.

This emancipation from sense perception is similar to what happened in mathematics at the beginning of the nineteenth century. At that time, geometries appeared in which parallel lines meet or in which there are no parallel lines at all. The angle sum of triangles in some of these geometries depended on their area. Algebras were constructed in which the almost obvious laws of numbers, for instance that 3 x 4 is equal to 4 x 3, did not apply.

In examining both nineteenth-century mathematics and twentieth-century physics, we see that we are only gradually becoming conscious of what we are actually doing in scientific research—and, for that matter, in any branch of learning. It becomes clear that we have learned to use concepts and ideas, on the one hand, and observations, on the other, independently of each other. Ideas can and do arise that are linked to each other without reference to observation.

Presumably there are ideas to fit all observations. Scientific research consists in finding these ideas. If they did not exist, science would be a futile undertaking. In contrast, however, it is true that not all ideas have sense-perceptible counterparts. (There are, for instance, ideas of justice for which such counterparts have yet to be created.) Mathematics is a discipline in which ideas are often developed that are closely linked to sense perception (albeit only those of the body senses), ideas such as addition and subtraction in arithmetic or length and angle in geometry. Nevertheless, upon examining these concepts more closely, mathematicians realized that they are special instances of much wider ideas. In this way mathematicians were led from the sense perceptible to mathematical structures that were not necessarily connected to observation. In some cases relevant observations were found later. For instance, Georg Riemann developed a non-Euclidean geometry in the nineteenth century that turned out to be just what was needed by Einstein to create a general mechanics applicable to all bodies, even those moving very fast. Such bodies were discovered—or produced—in the twentieth century.

If ideas and observations are initially independent of each other, the question arises as to how we can tell when an idea fits an observation. While the observations are measurements and the ideas are mathematical, relating the two is comparatively easy. When we say that Euclidean geometry fits measurements on the Earth, we mean something along the following lines. Suppose that in a survey we lay out a triangle and measure two of its sides and the angle between them to the accuracy achievable with the usual surveying instruments. Then we insert the measured values into a formula that is part of the structure of Euclidean geometry, and we calculate the length of the third side. When we measure the third side, we obtain a value agreeing with the one calculated, again to the accuracy obtainable with the usual surveying instruments. If we had used a formula belonging to another geometry, there might have been a discrepancy between the measured and calculated lengths of the third side. We would then have said that Euclidean geometry applies and the new geometry does not apply to ordinary measurements on Earth. Scientists are fond of mathematics and measurements just because it is relatively easy, by simply comparing numbers, to establish whether the mathematics fits the observations.

The freeing of thinking from sense constraints in modern science often led to a reversal of the sequence of events customary to the classical science that preceded it. Rather than trying to explain already observed phenomena, thought experiments were carried out in the theater of the mind in order to *discover* phenomena. (This is the counterpart in modern science to classical science's building of machines in the mind.) Then, to verify theory, empirical observations were carried out to search for the new phenomena predicted mathematically. In this process much of the submicroscopic world of the quantum and the megascopic world of relativity theory was constructed. (By naming different worlds we merely mean that different conditions and principles exist for manipulating objects. In particular, we do not mean to imply a system of worlds, especially when pictured spatially. The terms submicroscopic, macroscopic, and megascopic are used only to refer to the fact that the measures involved in these worlds are of vastly different orders of magnitude. Only the macroscopic is known through sense experience.)

It was largely unnoticed that a wholly new way of thinking, one could say a new human faculty, came into use in gaining a foothold in these new worlds. We refer here to the ability to sustain thinking unsupported by sense experience or mental pictures based on such experience. As was the case at the inception of classical science, the grounds for confidence in this endeavor were provided by experience with the mathematics of the previous centuries. The "pure" mathematics employed in the worlds of twentieth-century physics was gained through a way of thinking new in the evolution of the human mind. A new faculty for unfolding thought forms in a consistent step-by-step fashion entirely independent of sensory input was at work. Since the conceptual content of the new physics was directed at what was ultimately measurable, bodily-spatial aspects of reality were revealed in these new worlds. Within these limits, modern physics was a playground for the development and experience of a human capacity for thinking unsupported by sense experience.

Let us now return to the phenomenological science described in the last chapter. We will try to show how ideas can lead us from observation to observation, helping us integrate phenomena into connected, intelligible totalities. Where appropriate, our thinking can now reveal mathematical laws without the invention of underlying mechanisms.

From Nature to Knowledge

In the last chapter we saw how observations of reflections can lead us to a mathematical description. The relationship between tangible object space (where sight and touch coincide) and a purely visual space (created by reflection) was described as a simple geometrical transformation: to every point in one space there corresponds a point in the other, with the two points located on a line perpendicular to and equidistant from the mirror plane. The geometrical description led us to perform a simple experiment using identical cups, the result of which was as predicted by the mathematics. Note, however, that the geometrical transformation is reciprocal, while the "real" phenomenon is not. In reality, a space in which sight and touch agree must exist before the reflected space can arise.

When looking into the water itself a "lifting" effect was noted. More accurately, to every touchable object in the water there corresponded a visible object closer to the water's surface whose position depended upon the observer's location. The tangible object was not visible, and the visible object was not touchable. We again found a geometrical law, one that relates the touch space of the tangible with the sight space of the visible objects.

Thus, the observations made by sight and touch are linked by purely geometrical law. *No use is made of the concept of "light rays."* Provided light rays are regarded merely as auxiliary concepts and not as something real, there is no harm in using them together with the well-known laws of reflection and refraction. In fact, using the ray model of light in some calculations often saves time and energy. However, the purely mathematical description, while being very general and elegant, leaves us free. For instance, it accommodates a wave model as well as the ray model.

Inspired by peering into the dark portions of a lake, the portions unobscured by reflections, we showed in the previous chapter how the beginnings of a conceptual grasp of color can be gained through relatively simple observations. Relationships of sequence and complementarity were expressed through the use of a color circle's geometrical formalism. It is characteristic of such relationships that they lack quantitative measure. For one thing, colors are not specified exactly. According to the reductionist view, this is a consequence of the subjectivity of color. Color is not "real" in its own right. The laws concerned with the subjective perception of nature are, in the reductionist view, considered laws of psychology rather than physics. It is asserted that the objective reality of visual phenomena lies instead in understanding the nature and properties of light.

Physicists are not accustomed to making a distinction between color and light. They often naïvely think that color appearances are a straightforward consequence of the wavelengths of the illuminating and reflected light. The actual discrimination of color, however, involves an intricate complex of factors that has steadfastly defied mechanistic explanation and measurement.

The realm of color has a structure that is qualitatively mathematical. Relationships between hues can, as we have seen, be represented geometrically by a color circle. Hue cannot, however, be modeled by entities existing in space, such as waves or particles. The fact that physicists have been unable to imagine a spatial equivalent of color is the basis for their rejection of color as a real element of the physical world.

The Objectivist Worldview

In our naïve everyday experience we assume that the world as a coherent totality—including objects and their spatial relationships—is simply given to us through sense perception. We are quite unaware of our inner participation in apprehending the world. This commonly held, naïve assumption is the starting point for the considerations that ultimately lead to the objectivist worldview.

These considerations begin when critical inquiry is made into *how* this world is conveyed to our consciousness. Various aspects of the world are perceived in different ways. We can touch the trunk of a tree, for example. It offers resistance. We can push against it with all our strength; we can clasp its solid, round form; we can even climb it. Its reality, experienced directly through our own body, cannot be doubted. But what about its color? We perceive it at a distance. How is this possible? There must, we presume, be some *thing* that transmits the color from the tree's leaves and trunk to our eyes.

Color is thought to arise in human consciousness as a response to electromagnetic radiation that is pictured as energy waves moving through space. These waves, which we endow with the reality of physical objects, are thought to produce colored images of varying brightness in human observers and are therefore given the name "light." Since, however, in this view color is not present until the human being responds to this stimulus, the tree itself *cannot properly be said to be a particular color.*

In its examination of how human beings perceive the "given" world, habitual Western thought uncritically accepts bodily-spatial attributes as the objective reality. It is not possible, however, to account for the independent existence of the so-called secondary qualities within this "objective" bodily-spatial world.

Let us return to the objectivist view of the tree. According to this conception, the tree absorbs and reflects light in its own characteristic way. Such absorption and emission processes do not require color for their description, neither does the description of light radiation itself. Accordingly, color concepts must be introduced in order to describe the *experience of seeing* and not to describe what is, in the objectivist view, presumed to actually be there independent of seeing. The conclusion is inescapable that an unobserved tree is devoid of color. But how do we mentally picture an unobserved tree? Could a colorless tree be anything other than invisible?

Many readers will have recognized this conundrum as a visual version of the familiar problem of whether or not there is a sound in the forest if a tree falls with no one present to hear it. This problem usually presupposes that objective disturbances in the air act as stimuli to the ear, which are heard within human consciousness as sound. People are often impatient with such a discussion. It seems to be quibbling casuistry to make a distinction between the conditions that act as an acoustical stimulus and the sound actually heard. Nevertheless, we must insist on the distinction. A so-called acoustic pressure wave consists of contractions and expansions of air. Quite literally it requires nothing acoustic in its complete description, just as light waves require nothing visual in their description. Pressure waves are completely bodily-spatial in nature. The only acoustic aspect about pressure waves is that they are able to stimulate sound—but only if an observer is present to actually note the disturbance with ear and brain and mind!

If we inquire into how we conceive a given spatial world of discrete, solid objects within the objectivist conception, we cannot logically continue to picture such a reality to be anything other than silent, devoid of color, and neither hot nor cold. We cannot even picture it as dark. Birds do not sing, unless by singing we mean that they emit soundless song. Their feathers are neither vibrant nor dull of hue. There is no fragrance emanating from the flowers in the field in which they grow.

The conclusion is that within the objectivist conception, nature as we experience it cannot exist as a reality in an external world that is independent of human observers. According to the objectivist view, the only qualities that remain are the bodily-spatial ones, the ones that are tangible. An object such as a tree (or, alternatively, the atoms of which it is thought to be composed), the portion of electromagnetic radiation through which the visual presence of the tree is made known, and the pressure waves associated with the rustling of its leaves all boast of spatial extent as a distinguishing characteristic. This is not true, for example, of the greenness of the leaves or of the rustling itself. It is no accident, of course, that all this dovetails neatly with the fact that physical science has concerned itself solely with what is measurable and therefore spatial. Indeed, this limitation, together with the domination of the body senses, is primarily responsible for the contemporary view that reality consists only of things in space, completely independent of those beings who know of their existence.

In a way we have come full circle. Not only is a smile made grotesque by science and robbed of its human meaning (chapter one), but also *nature itself* is made meaningless when we limit reality to what is measurable and, therefore, spatial in character and experienced only through the body senses.

The Nature of the Physical World

Let us return to the naïve view of human experience from which the considerations leading to scientific objectivism take their start. Upon closer examination we realize that this common, everyday experience of reality is not simply given through sense perception but that it is already the *result* of our active, though largely unconscious inner participation. Everyday experience is by no means independent of our consciousness but is rather more or less permeated by it. The question cannot therefore be the one that, as we have just seen, inevitably leads to objectivism: "How is this world conveyed to our consciousness?" Inasmuch as what we naïvely presume to be the given world is, in fact, the end result of a cognitive process, the question to pose is: "How is our knowledge of the world constituted?"

In chapter two we began to answer this question by investigating the role played by our senses in acquiring knowledge of the world. We saw how the sense of touch helps us define separateness, how our somatic sense gives us the sensation of weight, how our senses of movement and balance are essential to our experience of space and so on. In a similar way, our sense of sight communicates shades of dark, light, and color, and our sense of hearing conveys sound. In and of themselves, however, these various senses impart nothing more than disparate sensations.

Examination of the process of cognition itself reveals that our knowledge of a tree, for example, arises as we establish meaningful relationships between diverse sensory perceptions through our *concept* of a tree. The sound we hear becomes meaningful as the "rustling of its leaves." The colors we see, the shapes we perceive, the resistance we feel all take on meaning in relation to this concept. The tree as we know it is the result of the active integration of various sense perceptions into a coherent conceptual-perceptual whole. Our knowledge of reality arises through the marriage of sense and thought. Sense perceptions alone, devoid of any conceptual relatedness, communicate neither objects nor spatial relationships. Henri Bortoft has described pure perception, an experience we can begin to approach only by willfully withdrawing all cognitive activity from perception, as a "state of awareness without meaning" [Bortoft 1996]. And yet without sense perception we could have no knowledge of the world.

We have shown (in chapter two) that the bodily-spatial world of physics is no less grounded in sense experience than are colors, sounds, tastes, smells, and so on. Surface, volume, mass, movement, and space derive their compelling character from the participation of our body senses: the touch, somatic, movement, and balance senses. Yet there is no reason to attribute reality to the volume, mass, and shape of the tree but to deny reality to its color and sound. Both aspects are known the same way. Without exception, all perceptual contents of the physical world, as we naïvely experience it, are mental conclusions derived from interpreting sense experience. Science's goal of knowledge, described from the point of view of passive observers cognizing a world from which they are separated, is not tenable. Specifically, the habitual objectivist view of reality described in the previous section is impossible. Yet this idea persists as the model for the human researcher's knowing witness to physical reality.

Lurking behind the idea of objective knowledge of a world separate from our own existence is our experience as cognizing beings that knowledge of the world is attainable. The edifice of science is strong evidence for such a conviction. But as we know, such knowledge has been limited to knowing bodily-spatial objects experienced as having an independent existence. This alone is usually called objective knowledge.

We perceive our own bodies, brains included, in the same way we perceive objects external to ourselves. Although the physical sense organs of human bodies—eyes, skin, nose, and so on—are required for perception, they cannot be said to perceive. It is the mind, making use of them, that perceives. The gulf bridged by cognition is not between our personal material bodies and external objects. It is the divide between the knowing mind and what is perceived, wherever it may be located. It is difficult to accept this idea because we customarily identify our own *selves* with our personal material bodies. Such an identification has its source within the body-sense bias of contemporary science, with its materialism, reductionism, and mechanism. This is also the reason for locating thinking within a material brain instead of a real, but nonmaterial mind. In having to re-cognize and give content to the mind as a reality and not just as an epiphenomenon of the material brain, we are brought back to that half of the Cartesian dichotomy, *res cogitans*, which has been ignored in favor of its material counterpart, *res extensa*. The intellectual realization that mind is just as real as material objects is not, of course, the same thing as the inward experience of it. Lip service alone will not free us from habitual materialism.

It is now apparent that the elements of the bodily-spatial world to which physics limits its consideration are objectively no more real—or less real—than the nonspatial sense percepts of which human beings are also aware. Or, to put it another way, color and sound are just as real as are physical form and weight. They deserve to be taken just as seriously. In the historical development of science, the inner experience of the certainty of knowing (associated with bodily-spatial perceptual world contents) has been confused and exclusively identified with the experience of the reality of physical objects. Our experience of certainty is based on the impression that measurement somehow removes an object from its dependence on the knowing human mind.

When, for example, an approaching baseball does not appear to the batter to grow larger, it is taken as evidence of the subjectivity of the human sense organization. We have the naïve confidence that the size and location of an object, such as a baseball, can be measured and that such a measurement is independent of our own selves. It may be that such a measurement can be carried out for the baseball, although it is no simple matter when it is moving! To understand the situation correctly, we must appreciate the difference between observing a directly oncoming object with one eye or with two. Moving a finger toward your nose and observing it with only one eye, you will see it increase in size as you would expect from the laws of perspective. Viewed with both eyes, however, the size of the finger does not change. In the first case, the finger is seen two dimensionally in perspective, as if it were a changing painting. In the second case, however, the finger is seen three dimensionally through the muscular cooperation of both eyes, each eye seeing a slightly different view. The latter case is the situation with the baseball. Attention is on the object itself rather than on the scene. The situation is similar to the problem experienced when the location of the refracted image of an object does not coincide with the location of its tangible perception (or, where we feel it to be). We simply bring thinking to bear, along with whatever sense perceptions are available, so as to order the situation in thought. Reality is this ordered understanding. In this way scientific knowledge is subject to constant elaboration and revision. Thus, reality becomes increasingly well known.

In the previous chapter we pointed to the inconsistency involved in asking such questions as "What is color really?" The implication is that color is something other than what it appears to be. The "something other" is presumed to be bodily-spatial in nature and is pictured to exist—wrongly as we have shown—independently of the questioner. We showed that science can be carried out without resort to bodily-spatial assumptions concerning the nature of reality. Instead, our only assumption was that physical reality consists of sense phenomena ordered by concepts appropriate to the phenomena. This bringing together of concepts and sense-perceptible manifestations *is* physical reality. It is the business of science to bring them together. In this we agree with Rudolf Steiner, who suggested that the split we experience between what comes to us through thinking and what comes to us through our senses is a consequence of the human organism [Steiner 1988]. The split is not an imperfection of the human being, but instead the basis for our freedom. A baby must first distinguish between itself and its surroundings before being able to use the word *I*. Our sense of being an independent individual can arise only through separation from the world. This separation is given through our unique constitution. The split between inner and outer experience forces us to work with pictures in our consciousness. Those pictures, being *only* pictures, do not have the coercive power of external reality. Hence we are free to distinguish and combine them as we wish without, initially at least, doing any harm. The scientific work of thinking with pictures educates us and helps us evolve new faculties. Cognition in the true sense is more than gaining information; it is an active participation in the world through which we develop new capacities.

While human beings experience the world in the form of a split between inner and outer, the world itself is whole. We are exposed to the whole of the world via the separate functions of thinking and of sensing. Thinking and sensing are, so to speak, our "paths" to the world. Being different ways, they are also the source of the split in our experience. The task of cognition is to heal that which has been split. We do this by reuniting concepts with their percepts. When a phenomenon is made whole in this way we no longer have questions concerning it. We know it in reality.

We maintain that a methodology of science free of assumptions, as outlined in the previous chapter, is adequate to apprehend physical reality in its completeness. This method is not limited to bodily-spatial elements, but the results of such methodology will be measurable when used on phenomena appropriate to measurement. However, since the methodology is not limited to such phenomena, it is capable of incorporating the fullness of nature into scientific understanding. Furthermore, the methodology is not limited to the physical world. It could, for example, be utilized to understand inner experience and thus to develop a phenomena-based psychology. We consider next how biology might be incorporated into a scientific worldview.

Biology As a Science of Life

One reason mythical renderings of natural phenomena seem quaint to us now is that personal, animate interventions are employed to explain inanimate, mechanical processes. Not until a clear distinction between living organisms and inanimate objects was made by the ancient Greeks was the genesis of science possible. It is surely one of history's ironies that the wresting of the concept of the inanimate from a world previously experienced as wholly

animate has led dangerously close to the world's being conceived as totally inanimate. Within the conceptions of contemporary biology there is no place for life. In the now
familiar pattern, biology treats life as an epiphenomenon of
ultimate realities that are bodily-spatial, reduced, and mechanistic. The current focus on genetic-molecular entities
exemplifies this trend. They enable us to explain functions
of organisms in terms of mechanisms. This way of thinking
is so successful that biological processes can be manipulated
and controlled in a very impressive fashion. In the process,
however, the wholeness of the organism is lost. Since the
very concept of organism implies totality, without wholeness
"organism" is an empty concept. Once this fact is recognized, we can begin to employ "living wholeness" as a rigorous concept within science.

   In ordinary experience, unburdened by scientific expectations, it is not difficult to recognize the presence of a living existence. Living matter grows, unlike crystals, which
increase in size only through the addition of material to
their surfaces—but not by growing. We regard growth as
expressive of an inner self-organizing formative principle.
Plant leaves in various stages of development are not difficult to arrange into the temporal sequence in which they
appeared. Such arrangements allow us to see each leaf as
an expression of a single living entity—a wall lettuce, as
shown in the accompanying figure, or perhaps a thistle.
Even missing leaves can be imaginatively supplied, whether
to fill in gaps left by uncollected leaves of the plant or even
to obtain leaf forms that had not yet appeared materially
in the plant. This is accomplished through the flexible
imaginative grasp of a totality already known in the form of
an intuition, not through building up leaf shapes by add-
ing together reduced elements.

In other words, the concept "inner self-organizing formative principle" is that which allows us to see a particular leaf as an expression of a potential for continuously evolving forms, that is, to see it as being alive rather than as a static picture or a member of a sequence of forms. It is only within this mobile conception of continuous change that the leaf developments pictured are to be understood. It is this concept that allows us to distinguish the leaf of an artificial plant from that of a living one, even if we have to touch the leaves in order to distinguish which concept is appropriate, that of a living plant or that of an object of artifice.

Recognizing the futility of trying to derive organic forms from reduced elements, some biologists have postulated the existence of a "field of form." This has led a number of biologists to employ the mathematics of chaos and complexity in an attempt to gain a theory of form as an emergent property of organisms viewed as complex dynamic systems (rather than arrangements of smaller components). Somewhat analogous to the physicist's field of force, but much more dynamic, biological fields of form are conceived as self-organizing totalities that superintend the transformation of organic matter into evolving shapes of living material bodies. The biologist Brian Goodwin, for example, has

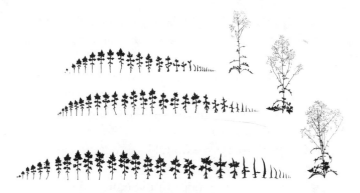

ventured to understand the discrete steps of evolution evident in the increasingly complex forms of vertebrate limb structure (from phalange through metatarsals to tarsal) or in giant green unicellular algae (from whorls arrayed on a stem to a cap). In Goodwin's approach, particular forms emerge out of complex dynamic interactions between individual states of the field and distinct, but growing shapes of the organism. Form and field tend to reinforce each other in stable (but dynamic) relationships that serve to generate the conditions for the further appearance of new forms as the organism grows [Goodwin 1994].

In a rather different approach, both mathematically and conceptually, Lawrence Edwards used projective geometry to construct families of curves and surfaces that exhibit striking similarities to the forms of flower buds, seed cones, and even beating hearts [Edwards 1982]. The forms arise from the simplest movements of points, lines, and planes in space. In principle, no measurements are necessary to make the constructions. Thus, organic forms can be seen to arise out of the qualitative properties of the simplest elements of geometry. Measurables appear, in Edward's work, only with the finished organic form. They do not regulate it.

It is not our purpose here to discuss theories of biological form in detail or to judge their adequacy for explaining the phenomena. We only wish to point out that if and when a forming principle that embraces a living organism in its entirety is apprehended, such a principle will be *just as much a part of the reality of the organism* as its physical parts. Bearing in mind that it is an illusion to expect to know real entities independent of thinking, we would like once again to stress that, for us as cognizing human beings, the reality of a natural object consists of the totality of the entity's impressions, both the concepts we see through the window of thought and the percepts seen through the window of the senses.

It is our conviction that any endeavor resting exclusively on mathematical formalism will not be entirely adequate to grasp the intrinsic nature of biological forming entities. This conviction rests on the realization that to perceive an entity such as a plant as living, it is necessary to be able to actually see its form within a context of continuous development and not as a discrete sequence of finished shapes. In other words, *life* is always within a context of *becoming*. It is the thought of continuous becoming that allows us to distinguish between living and nonliving material form. It is this concept married to its corresponding sense basis that constitutes the reality of life.

Nevertheless, purely formal mathematical methods such as Goodwin's do guard against the danger of imaginative vagueness. Formal mathematics here plays its historic scientific role of providing a ground of certainty to support further development of human thought. However, it is possible to let go of the scaffolding of formal mathematics in favor of a more inward participation in the growth process while remaining conceptually rigorous and retaining an objective corrective to possible conceptual errors.

Jochen Bockemühl has made some very promising beginnings in this direction [Bockemühl 1981]. He has shown that the "flexible picturing" through which we recognize that a sequence of leaf forms belongs to a single plant, or through which we recognize an anomaly where a caterpillar has eaten a piece from a leaf, is also able to explain the relationship of the plant to the environment in which it grows. The individual plant expresses not only its type but also, through its leaf formation, the soil, water, air, light, and warmth conditions within which it grew. For example, an observer who knows a type through imaginative faculties enhanced to "flexible picturing" is able to recognize, in the "outspokenness" of its leaf forms, that an individual plant has grown in conditions of strong light. The three wall lettuces shown on the right of the previous figure were grown in direct sunlight while those on the left were grown in the shade, the upper plants having been seeded earlier than the lower ones. The leaves of the plants grown in sunlight are distinguished from the leaves of the shade plants by a high degree of sharply edged, fine segmentation. The individuation of the leaves of the wall lettuces grown in the sunlight is also expressed by distinctive coloring. Yellow intrudes on the green of their leaves, which are distinctively tinged with borders of different shades of red. In contrast, the leaves of the shade-grown plants are a uniform green.

Bockemühl refers to the essence of light as an agent that "brings to appearance." Such a concept of light, together with a precise understanding of "living wholeness" of leaves attainable for any given species through flexible picturing, could be considered proper elements of a new biology. This is especially so since this concept is completely consistent with what we have deduced concerning the nature of light in a purely physical, nonbiological, context. (In physics, light also "brings to appearance," but in the sense of our usual visual understanding.)

From the materialistic standpoint it might appear that imagination used for direct participation with nature rather than for gaining an intermediary mathematical model is fraught with the danger of vagueness and subjectivity following from the qualitative and individual nature of imaginativeness. This type of objection, however, begs the question. As we have already seen, the entire world of phenomena is an "image" known through the participation of human mental activity. Overcoming the danger of vagueness and subjectivity is a matter of our willingness to be conscious of the relationship between our imagination and the phenomenal world and to act accordingly. The authenticity of our mental pictures can be verified through experiment. As we have seen, plants grown under different environmental conditions can be compared with the pictures created by our thinking.

So far we have considered how the holistic entity "plant type" is rendered intelligible through its leaf development and how that entity is acted upon by the environment. As Bockemühl points out, knowledge on this level is not sufficient for an understanding of the continuity preserved through a deeper metamorphosis. Spatial description alone is of little help in understanding the transition from leaves to flowers. Furthermore, since environmental conditions do not affect essential flower characteristics, they are also of no aid. What is needed here, according to Bockemühl, is an intuitive discernment of the "inner gesture," the essential quality that informs the totality of leaf transformations and especially the appearance of the flower.

In previous chapters we developed a way of "doing science" without abstract physical models. In keeping with that discussion, the science of biology, liberated from physics, can also be seen in a very different light. We are free to search for concepts appropriate to and taken from the realm of biology. Such an undertaking requires observation guided by intuitive thinking, together with concrete imaginative participation in individual biological phenomena. In this way we are able to recognize plants as alive. The reality of the plant is, literally, the whole that consists of its sensible manifestation in space united with the imaginative concept of continuous becoming. Thus, we formulate a concept that actualizes our perception of the plant as living. In addition, we can find an appropriate concept for the essential quality, or "inner gesture," which manifests in every aspect of the plant but expresses itself most strongly in its blossom. Remembering "the smile" we met at the beginning of this book, we can now see clearly the nature of the problem that arose when we tried to describe a smile scientifically. The human essence of the smile was lost because the science used was limited to methods of description appropriate only to physical reality and, moreover, to a reality only bodily-spatial in character.

We believe our study has shown that there is nothing inherent in the nature of science that would limit it to concepts and methods drawn from the physical world alone. Just as biology must be appropriately based on truly biological considerations, so, too, we would expect a legitimate psychology to rest on concepts appropriate to the human realm. Recognizing that the boundaries historically placed upon such a program were unwarranted, we can now discover hope.

Holism

Modern natural science has, of course, evolved from a genuine search for truth. Its pioneers strove to transcend the subjective view of the world conveyed to them through their senses. Impressed by the intersubjective nature of mathematics, they evolved in due course the reductionistic method we have today. It has become natural to equate scientific understanding with successful reductionistic explanation. Beyond mere satisfaction for the intellect, such explanations have given rise to novel technologies through which practically all realms of nature can be manipulated. This power of manipulation is cited as the strongest proof of the reductionistic doctrine.

On the other hand, the growing problems of contemporary civilization have led to a call for holism. By taking the whole to be the sum of its parts, the reductionistic method has been leading humanity into chaos. Perhaps an objective science that takes the world apart only to reassemble it with the aid of ever larger computers does not lead to a rational view of the world after all?

In this book we have suggested that human beings need not fear the subjective nature of their senses. We have proposed that different realms be understood with concepts appropriate to their phenomena. Now the question might be asked, In doing this will we not get innumerable "sciences" according to the distinctiveness of the experience of each individual? Will science degenerate into a doubly subjective enterprise based merely on the human faculties of perception and of thought? Were not the examples in chapter four less a description of objects than a narrative about associated perceptions and thoughts, that is, mere subjective personal experiences?

Our answer to these questions involves the acknowledgment of the danger. Of course, human sense organs are self-centered and not always reliable. But denying the reality they convey to us does not solve the problem. Our proposal is that we should develop our faculties of sensing and thinking (including "precise imagination") so as to become increasingly versatile. In this way we can move to a less self-centered, less subjective view of the world.

What is a self-centered view of the world? A comparison with animals helps us here. Any serious attempt to understand a species will take into account their relationship to their surroundings. Animals are very specialized. They have faculties known as the instincts of their species—the beaver can bite through wood, and spiders can spin a thread. Their faculties enable them to create their habitat—the beaver building dams, the spider weaving its net. Animals change from one behavioral mode to another according to their surroundings. Birds form a group to migrate seasonally, and they intermittently shift from singing to searching for food. Animals respond instinctively to the appearance of specific objects in their environment; a mouse, for example, calls forth the cat's desire. Because each species of animal is highly specialized, it can have nothing other than a subjective view of the world. In this sense animals are the specialists who are unable to unite in mutual scientific and cultural striving. Human beings are not specialized to such an extent. At the very least, they can become conscious of any specialization in other human beings (if not of their own).

Looking at the same landscape, a geologist, a real estate agent, and a soldier may see its traits in quite different ways. They apply different concepts that enable them to see the possibilities for different activities. Longtime residents of the area may very well see mining operations, housing developments, or troop movements as detrimental to the life they have been leading there. We all employ concepts gained from experience in our own field of life. However, to the extent that they base their perceptions of possible future action solely on specialized experience, the soldier, geologist, and real estate broker can be said to have surrendered individual judgment for the sake of group egoism. Being self-centered carries the danger of obstructing one's openness to the experience of percepts that may reveal new possibilities for creating the future.

Human specialization in the realm of thought is by no means insurmountable. We can learn from others and thereby increase our versatility as thinkers. It is through this process of listening to each other that we can become aware of our own subjectivity; interest in other people introduces us to new ideas.

Interest in several areas will enhance our understanding of any single realm. Of course, the study of plants leads to a greater understanding of plants, and the observation and study of children will lead to a greater understanding of children. But one's concept of development will be deepened through observation and study of both plants and children. The more experience we have, the greater will be our appreciation for the new realms we encounter. We are more able to form ideas that bring the realms of nature into relation with each other.

Certainly, a truly scientific approach must be appropriate to the object of study. This means that scientists must learn to acquire the faculties appropriate to any object they may seek to understand. The totality of world contents can be understood as the object that requires the ultimate faculties for which we may strive.

Morality and Choice in Science

Human beings are creating a world that is increasingly inhospitable to themselves or anything else alive. The empathetic basis on which we relate to nature is eroded, as is that on which we relate to each other and to our own selves. Our impotence to reverse these trends derives from our unquestioning acceptance of the hypothetical-reductive-mathematical methods of science. We seem to feel that such methods are logically necessary. Reductionists are convinced that objective knowledge can be gained by no other means. However, built into these methods is the unsupported presupposition of a reality that, in its finality, is static, fragmented, and impersonal. Within such a reality there is no place for life or sentient beings.

Even people aware of these difficulties and possessing a healthy sense for life find themselves unable to act in ways that are integrated with their humanity. Professional ecologists, for example, personally relate to nature out of an innate sense for its wholeness. It is usually this awareness that initially drew them to pursue their scientific studies. But "wholeness of life" does not have the status of reality either within the scientific community or in public life. Thus, ecologists cast their investigations in purely economic terms, hoping that monetary values can influence public policy and save nature from destruction. But this approach is wrong on two counts. For ecologists themselves it is self-destructive because of the fundamental personal untruth. Furthermore, it supports the idea that economic gain should be the primary motivating factor in our relationship to the natural world and to one another.

We could list innumerable similar examples of people working in ways that increase fragmentation while they themselves inwardly sense that something is fundamentally wrong. Instead, we would like to suggest the reason few people take the risks required to change this situation: deep down they feel that it is scientifically impossible to justify any ultimate reality other than one of impersonal building blocks. Despite its inner longings the modern psyche embraces the contemporary materialistic worldview of science on some level. Perhaps we feel that the price of its abandonment would be the loss of our self-identity. Sadly, it is now clear that the selfhood we would preserve is gradually being permeated by a sense of meaninglessness that is the real price of our continuing to think in the framework of the modern worldview.

In spite of all this, the materialistic worldview is untenable in the face of the evidence. As we have noted, science has occupied itself with only a very proscribed aspect of reality. The usual justification for this limitation is unsustainable once the role played by the body senses in science is understood. The stumbling block to a new scientific worldview—that is, the inability to conceive of an alternate methodology of science, one neither reductionist nor arbitrarily limiting sense experience—we have shown to be surmountable by employing the methods of the previous chapter.

It is a great challenge to someone steeped in customary scientific training to recognize these new methods as scientific. One must come to believe that mathematical rigor of thinking does not automatically require symbolic formalism. For many, this trust seems to entail stepping off the solid ground that supports our thinking and entering into a kind of mental swimming. But only in this way can the investigator gain life, wholeness, and meaning within science.

The form and the spirit of the questions asked specify the nature and contexts of permissible answers. The goal of recovering the reality of nature within scientific description can be achieved only in the context of wholeness. This means that we must search for and investigate the most important aspects of phenomena directly perceptible to us rather than lose ourselves in the pseudophenomena characteristic of the usual reductionistic methods.

We must recognize that choice is possible. Do we wish to involve ourselves with the world of phenomena, with nature as a whole, or do we wish to fathom the microscopic world with its atomic, fragmented character? The two worlds are concurrent and distinct. Either path can be pursued. The path we choose has far-reaching consequences for humanity. It is literally true that we create and are responsible for the reality in which we live. Uniting ourselves with phenomena will tend to unify humanity and bring wholeness to nature. If we choose reductionism, not only nature but society too will be reduced, fragmented. We can no longer use the fiction that science is value-neutral in order to escape our responsibility. The practice of science, the nature of our questions, carries with it, from its very inception, a moral choice and a moral responsibility. The morality of science is not simply a matter of how results are used! Furthermore, since nature and humanity are inseparable, their evolution is also inseparable.

Just as personal isolation and alienation are the inevitable fruits of preoccupation with the microscopic atomic world, so do union and belonging surely follow from scientific concern with phenomena along the lines we have sketched. The first choice required our cultivation of the quality of detachment from phenomena while at the same time calling for passionate participation in the inner activity of cognizing. The second choice calls for actively attending to and participating in phenomena. And just those qualities that enable us to participate in phenomena—selfless interest and involvement in the single, individual, specific other—make for a healthy social life and rich interpersonal relations.

The practice of science yields both outer and inner results. Detachment from phenomena, as cultivated in the past few centuries, has led to our mastery of the material world manifested in machines and structures. It has also given us our sense of individuality and freedom, that is, an inner kind of detachment. Surely we do not want to give up such fruits of science. But just as surely, its price, alienation from the phenomenal world and meaninglessness of life, is unacceptable. Only a science that can conceive of a wholeness in which each part is an expression of the unity of the whole will be able to solve the increasingly difficult problems that face humanity. Furthermore, practicing the intense imaginative participation required of such a science will develop the attitudes and capabilities needed to heal the sicknesses that result from living in a technologically advanced society. We must not lose the freedom and sense of individuality acquired by reductionistic science, but they must be supplemented by the capabilities generated through the holistic approach. Working together, both are required of us if we are to be free and, out of this freedom, to bring love to the world.

Bibliography

BARFIELD, O., *Saving the Appearances: A Study in Idolatry*, 2nd ed., Wesleyan Univ. Press, Middletown, Connecticut (1988).

BOCKEMÜHL, J., *In Partnership with Nature*, Bio-dynamic Literature, Wyoming, R.I. (1981).

BORTOFT, H., *The Wholeness of Nature: Goethe's Way toward a Science of Conscious Participation in Nature*, Lindisfarne Press, Hudson, N.Y. (1996).

DRAKE, S., *Discoveries and Opinions of Galileo*, Doubleday Anchor Books, Garden City, N.Y.(1957).

EDWARDS, L., *The Field of Form*, Floris Books, Edinburgh, Scotland(1982).

GOODWIN, B.C., *How the Leopard Changed Its Spots: The Evolution of Complexity*, Scribner, N. Y. (1994).

LOCKE, J., *An Essay Concerning Human Understanding*, Book II, Chapter VIII, London (1689).

STEINER, R., *The Science of Knowing*, Mercury Press, Spring Valley, N.Y. (1988). See also *Intuitive Thinking as a Spiritual Path: A Philosophy of Freedom*, Anthroposophic Press, Hudson, N.Y. (1995).

Index

and inner world split, 9-12, 15-
19, 123-124
knowledge of, 118-124
objectivist view of, 113-118
scientific view of, 51-53, 125
self-centered view of, 132-134
sensory experience of, 22-23, 24-
26, 29, 30-31, 34, 92-93, 116

P
Particles, 14-15, 60, 68, 110
particle-wave paradox, 64-65, 104-
105
Pauli exclusion principle, 95
Personal activity, in science, 6-8
Perspective
laws of, 84, 122
in reflection, 82-83
Philosophy, 21, 51
corpuscular, 38, 40, 52-53
"natural philosophy," 54-56
Photochemistry, 63-65, 96-97, 100-
105
Photoelectric effect, 62-63, 102
Photon, 63-65, 103
Physics, 13-14, 29, 95, 100, 106, 115,
121, 130, *See also* Science
applied, 22-23, 29-30
bodily-spatial bias of, 120
classical, 22, 61, 66, 68, 70
"generalized coordinates," 96-97
high-energy, 14-15
mathematical, 108-113
of reflection, 84-85
Piaget, Jean, 22
Pictures. *See* Flexible picturing;
Mental pictures
Planck, Max, 62-63, 71
Planets, motion of, 39, 45-46, 48-50
Plants, 5, 125-131
Plato, 21, 45
Pre-science, 13-14, 38, 53
Psychology, 13, 115, 124, 131
Ptolemy, 46
Pythagoras, 20-21, 39

Q
Quanta, 62, 112
of energy, 14, 110
of light, 97, 102-105

Quantum mechanics, 69, 105
Quantum theory, 62-66, 70-71

R
Radiation, 103-105, 116
Radioactivity, 62
Reality
bodily-spatial, 118-124
creation of, 136-138
materialistic, 13-14, 106
of nature, 89-90, 118-120, 126-131
Reductionism, 13, 15, 107, 121, 131-
132, 134-136
Reflection, 63, 80-88, 113-114
Reformation, 38, 47
Refraction, 114, 122
color and, 86-88
Relativity theory, 112
and ordinary thinking, 66-71
Religion, 16, 21, 39, 43-44, 46-47, 51
Renaissance, 38, 43
Retina, 32-33, 96, *See also* Eye; Vision
Riemann, George, 111
Rods and cones, 32

S
Scholars, 19-22, 35-41, 43
Schumacher, E.F., 10
Science, 3-8, *See also* Classical
science; Mathematics; Physics
applied, 84-85
bodily-spatial bias of, 113-123
compared to sensory experience,
42-43
dehumanizing force of, 2, 10-12,
106-108, 126-138
"doing science," 130-131
experiential basis for, 17-18
materialist basis of, 106-108
mathematical reduction in,
111-112
morality and choice in, 134-138
pre-science, 13-14, 38, 53
as religion, 16
significance determination in,
18-19
Scientific equilibrium, 73, 84
Self
alienation of, 11, 51-54
experience of, 7, 121, 135-136

Also in This Series

THE WHOLENESS OF NATURE
Goethe's Way toward a Science of
Conscious Participation in Nature
by Henri Bortoft

In this major work, Bortoft masterfully articulates the difference between Goethe's approach and that of mainstream science. Whereas conventional science analyzes phenomena and seeks to explain them in terms of their material components, the Goethean approach investigates how the whole is revealed in each of its parts. Bortoft shows how Goethe's scientific method opens the way toward a dynamic, qualitative understanding of nature in its interrelatedness and wholeness, thereby providing a much needed complement to the reductive, quantitative methods of modern science.

The book includes Bortoft's earlier essays *Goethe's Scientific Consciousness* and *Counterfeit and Authentic Wholes.* The main body of the work, *Understanding Goethe'e Way* of *Science,* consists of a further lively elucidation of Goethe's method and places it into the historical context of modern science.

GENETICS AND THE MANIPULATION OF LIFE:
The Forgotten Factor of Context
by Craig Holdrege

This very readable, informative work begins with striking examples of the plasticity of plants as they develop in response to their environment. Holdrege then describes how Gregor Mendel set out on a path of reduction, which led ultimately to the popular belief that DNA must contain the information that determines every aspect of the organism. Closer examination reveals, however, that this information, projected into the DNA, emerges only when the DNA is seen in the light of its context within the organism as a whole.

By placing genetics back into the full context of life, Holdrege provides a much needed reality check in a field that may determine the future of life on earth, but in which our understanding lags far behind our ability to act.

Hans Gebert, Georg Maier, and Stephen Edelglass working in the Adirondacks

STEPHEN EDELGLASS is director of science at the Three-fold Educational Foundation in Chestnut Ridge, New York. His research and teaching (at the Green Meadow Waldorf School and Sunbridge College) is concerned with phenomena-based scientific methodology. For many years he was on the faculty of the Cooper Union for the Advancement of Science and Art in New York City. GEORG MAIER currently directs research into modes of observation and conceptualization of nature at the Forschungslinstitut am Goetheanum in Dornach, Switzerland. Formerly he was engaged in neutron diffraction research at the Kernforschungsanlage Jülich (KFA) in Germany. The late HANS GEBERT was co-director of the Waldorf Institute of Mercy College in Detroit, Michigan. Before that he was the director of the physics laboratory of the Birmingham Technical University in England. The late JOHN DAVY was vice-principal of Emerson College in Forest Row, England, after a long tenure as the science editor of the *Observer.*